NICOLA McINTOSH

CRYSTAL GRID
SECRETS

Learn the ancient mysticism
of sacred geometry

ROCKPOOL
PUBLISHING

A Rockpool book

PO Box 252

Summer Hill NSW 2130

rockpoolpublishing.com.au

facebook.com/RockpoolPublishing

ISBN 978-1-925682-07-6

Copyright text © Nicola McIntosh 2019

Copyright design © Rockpool Publishing 2019

Edited by Lisa Macken

Cover design by Jessica Le, Rockpool Publishing

Internal design and typesetting by Sara Lindberg, Rockpool Publishing

All images by Nicola McIntosh except for the following:

Page 6, 8, 13, 17, 18, 22, 35, 48, 58, 156, 157 and 183 by Shutterstock.

Page 2, 15, 26, 42, 56, 76, 99, 102, 127, 130, 149, 153, 173, 176, 194 and 196 by Skybox Creative and Unsplash.

A catalogue record for this book is available from the National Library of Australia

Printed and bound in China

10 9 8 7 6 5 4 3 2 1

CONTENTS

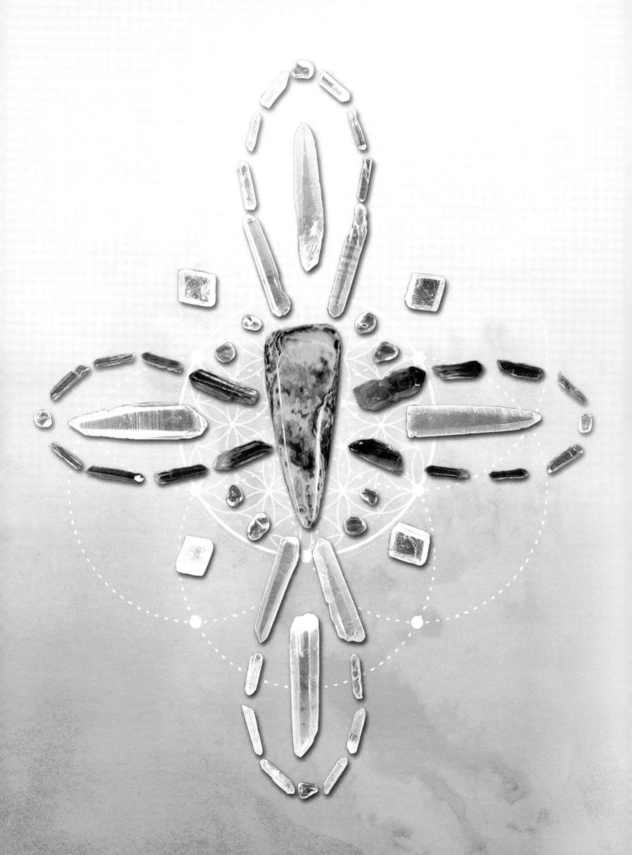

INTRODUCTION

At this book's outset I had already begun my shamanic path. For me, it was a chance to not only produce the book I had longed to write since I was a child, but also an opportunity to document my journey so I could create a path others could follow. I trust my intuition implicitly, which is how I know shamanism is a part of me. I haven't chosen this path to pick a name for myself. This path revealed itself to me and it became a remembrance of who I once was and who I am once again in this lifetime.

When I started writing this book I was working in an office as a personal assistant four days a week. I was an everyday office worker who did the daily grind in a 37-storey building with up to 200 people and computers on every floor. I sat in the daily peak-hour traffic longing to get home; nights consisted of making dinner, getting everything ready for the next day, watching a little TV and having an early night. Walking a shamanic path sometimes seemed like a romanticised view of how I would like to live, and I had contemplated that it could just be a daydream that gave me a brief lift out of the mundane. I am a very logical person, and who was I to think that I could walk the shamanic path? I mean, I was *just* an assistant … and there you have it: *'just'* was my way of keeping myself small. I felt my office title was nothing compared to that of everyone around me who I worked with, even though I was older than my boss.

Sometimes we keep ourselves small due to our own insecurities and perceptions about ourselves. We are in a constant state of comparing ourselves to others. I knew there had to be more to this life than eat, work, eat, sleep, eat, work … *zzzzzz*. I was a shell of a person rocking up to work each day. Sometimes I was so over doing what I was doing I would head to the bathroom, have a cry and then head back to my desk to pretend everything was normal. I didn't know how to change things or where to start. I sure as hell didn't have the money or the time to do anything I wanted because I was living from pay cheque to pay cheque. I have also had chronic health issues since I was kid, so I was constantly fatigued, in pain, lacking any kind of fulfilment in my life and caught in a cycle I thought was insurmountable.

Then I started working with my crystals again. I had been collecting rocks and crystals from a young age and never knew why I was so drawn to them. This also coincided with moving to a new home and having a beautiful park to walk through full of streams, rock faces and trees. A change started to happen the more I walked in nature and the more I started collecting and working with my crystals. I felt a sense of peace and enjoyment in what I was doing. My beautiful friend from work, Deena, shared my passion for crystals and we went on to create our online business Spirit Stone. Deena left to begin her own beautiful business, Spirit Weaver, and I continued to grow my business.

This new life started to snowball, and it wasn't long before I stumbled across crystal grids. I researched everything about them. My life started to shift dramatically, my relationship ended and I found myself living at Tamborine Mountain. This meant a two-hour commute to work each morning and then the same to go home, but now I had purpose. I always remember the statement that if you want to learn something well you should teach it, so I set about creating my online course in manifesting with crystal grids.

> *'Sometimes we keep ourselves small due to our own insecurities and perceptions about ourselves. We are in a constant state of comparing ourselves to others.'*

When I started researching for my course I felt as though my mind had been blown wide open. Everything just made such perfect sense, and then each day I would receive more and more pieces of the puzzle. I couldn't believe what I had stumbled on to, and it became obvious that this also had to go into a book. I worked on my book around the clock: on the train to work, in my lunch break, on the train back home and then until I went to bed and all through the weekend. Okay, yes, probably I went overboard and, yes, I am prone to burnout for this personality trait, but I thought this information just couldn't wait. I must get it out there; I have to help others see that there is more to this life!

I began to understand the gravity of putting a whole book together and the process became overwhelming, coupled with the fact I was still working and life on the mountain was proving harder than anticipated. I decided to keep plodding along with the book but to now also focus on creating my oracle deck, the *Crystal Grid Oracle*. It became obvious to me that this should come first. I needed to experience first-hand the powers of crystal grids and the energy that works through them, and what I learned from this oracle has given me complete faith in their energy.

My dream of becoming a published author also came true, following a redundancy at work that allowed me to focus on my Spirit Stone business and cards. It was another sign that I was now being supported because I was showing up regardless of the outcome. Trust me, it hasn't been easy by any stretch of the imagination, but when you trust your intuition implicitly you need to keep going, even if it is two steps forward and one step back.

WHAT IS A SHAMAN?

What exactly is a shaman? The first image that comes to my mind is a Native American or South American mature male with long grey hair dressed in leathers, with a headdress, a long staff with animal things hanging off everywhere and a leather bag full of stones and odd bits of stuff. It is someone living by themselves out in nature, such as in a desert or forest, who chants around a fire at night and lives alone.

Nope, doesn't sound like me; that is *not* what I am trying to achieve. As much as I would have loved to have been born this lifetime into that, I believe there is a way of being a modern-day shaman: living and respecting how a shaman thinks, feels and acts but with the ability to live in a modern surrounding among everyday people. Keep in mind that you can utilise shamanic practices, but this doesn't necessarily mean you are a shaman. When you are one you know, and the ego is stripped away of the need to proclaim yourself as one.

The Free Dictionary (an online resource) defines a shaman as: 'A member of certain tribal societies who acts as a medium between the visible world and an invisible spirit world and who practices magic or sorcery for purposes of healing, divination and control over natural events.'

Brian Froud (the illustrator for the movie *The Dark Crystal*) quotes: 'Artists are Shamans. They travel to the otherworld to bring back their images for everyone to see.'

My definition after researching and practising, is that shamanism is not a religion; it is a spiritual practice. It is about attuning yourself to nature's cycles and seeing the world through a different set of eyes. It is about allowing yourself to interact with everything on an energetic level, therefore understanding how everything is connected. It allows you to comprehend that there are other worlds with intelligent life forms coexisting around you. It is like taking off the blinkers of logical constraint and allowing yourself to see the kaleidoscope of energetic patterns that make up everything, which leads back to source – which ultimately is Source. This is why shamans are referred to as having one foot in both worlds: they bridge the gap between the physical and non-physical realities. They are individuals who can convey messages from the other worlds into this reality in a language this world can understand.

CELTIC SHAMANISM

There are many forms of shamanism around the world and each have their own deities and totem animals, but all have common traits that link them. As mentioned earlier, shamanism is not a religion; it is a spiritual practice. It can be practised alongside any religion or not encompass religion at all. It is not about worship, but is about respect for nature and every living creature on earth. It is about becoming one with nature's cycles and learning that we are a part of everything. Spirit resides in every living creature on this planet, and shamans believe we can communicate with all living beings because we are all created by spirit and are spirit. I feel that people can view shamans as having a special ability. My belief is that anyone is capable of this, but as a species we have forgotten how to do it.

Why have I chosen Celtic shamanism? Maybe due to being of Scottish descent I was drawn to it; ancestrally, it is in my blood. I cannot describe it, but I have always felt drawn to my heritage. As I looked into Celtic shamanism more and more it made so much sense to me. I really resonated with the teachings.

The Celts are recognised as being from Ireland, Scotland, England and Wales; however, many Celts came from all over Europe and incorporated their own practices with those of the indigenous people of the United Kingdom. The Celts themselves actually never used the word 'shamanism'. They called such people 'walkers between the worlds'. They were seen as being interpreters of the spirit realms. In other countries shamans are described as 'having one foot in both worlds', which again indicates their ability to communicate with other realms. A natural gift for many Celts, second sight (*da shealladh*) enabled a person to have visions, strong intuition and divinatory abilities, and was another way they could communicate with other-world beings.

Western society seems to have lost a significant portion of the knowledge our ancestors once knew, knowledge that allowed our ancestors to understand the workings of nature and our part in it. They knew they were not separate from the world around them but were part of it. They worked in harmony, and if only there had not been such a disruption in their practices I can only imagine where we would be now. This knowledge is still practised in many indigenous cultures around the world. Regardless of which continent they are from the indigenes have many common practices, but most importantly they have respect for all of nature and creation both big and small.

As torrid as our history is, with the desecration of certain cultures and things such as the witch trials, there is nothing we can do to change what has been done. The only thing we can do is realise we are in a modern society in which times and views are radically changing, and it is now a safe time to bring back the old ways and respect all cultures and life on this earth. In saying that, we do not need to be constrained in exactly how these old ways are practised; it's about taking the knowledge we do have and creating a new vision for the modern world.

I feel there are no longer enough healers on this earth to make the difference that is needed. It is time for the healers to become teachers and empower others to take their spiritual growth into their own hands, to help them navigate and understand the workings of nature so they can use their knowledge to help themselves and teach their children. This needs to happen on a mass scale to bring the balance back to earth before there is no turning back. People are beginning to understand the importance of this, and are becoming more awake and aware.

What I offer in these pages is my view of the world. Take what you need and believe what you may. All I can say is that through what I have learnt my life is becoming magical. I understand now how everything is connected in this intricate web of life, and how to manifest what you need once you have found your purpose, if you are willing to do the physical work it takes to make it a reality. Each day I feel more and more grateful for my connection to everything, for my understanding of the world. It has opened my eyes so much that I strongly feel I need to be heard. I wish for others to experience the amazing journey home I have experienced. I understand the struggles of everyday life and have finally found the path out of the fog. I know it is my purpose in this lifetime to help others find their way.

There is no single path we are all meant to take, so take what resonates with you from this book. Let your intuition guide you always.

MANIFESTATION

One common practice that can be witnessed through shamanism, witchcraft or religion is the power of ritual. Rituals can take many forms, from simple things such as lighting incense and placing it on an altar every morning to elaborate rituals that require the gathering of the right herbs, wearing specific jewellery, placing markings on your body and choosing the right planet alignments.

Why are we drawn to creating rituals, and what purpose do they serve in this day and age? Put simply, rituals are a way to focus your intent on a desired outcome. We all know about the law of attraction: what we send out is what we will in turn receive. Pretty simple, right? No one ritual is better than another; they all serve a purpose, and it is all about manifestation of some shape or form. Some rituals are performed to celebrate certain events but generally they serve a purpose of manifestation, whether we are asking for information, love or communication with spirits or whatever it may be.

This book is specifically about manifesting with crystal grids, mostly because I love crystals but also because I feel is it is a very relevant medicine coming to light in this modern day. Not only do they look beautiful, but they are fun to make and they work!

My intention with this book is to give you the necessary information to guide you in making your own grids, strengthening your communication abilities with your clair-senses and helping you manifest what you wish to create in your life. All of these skills essentially guide you back to your own connection to Source, because only you can do that. You need to find your own way.

Where do you start? By asking yourself: 'What do I want my life to look like? What do I term as living a successful life?' If you don't really know what you want, then how is the universe meant to bring it to you? So let's start at the beginning .

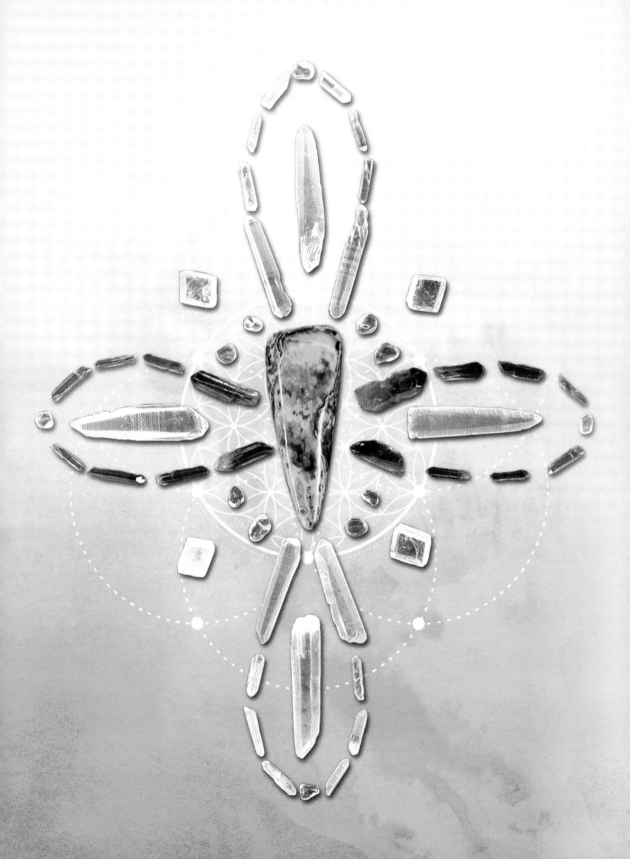

CHAPTER 1

SOURCE

'There is nothing solid in the universe. Everything takes up form by its vibration.'

Source is the term I give to the energy that creates all life; that is all life, the all that is, or God if you like to name it thus. Source is what gives us life, but it is possibly something that cannot be fully understood until we depart from this world. I feel it is so beyond human comprehension it is impossible to grasp. When I talk about connecting to Source I am trying to explain the way in which we can gain a deeper understanding of ourselves,

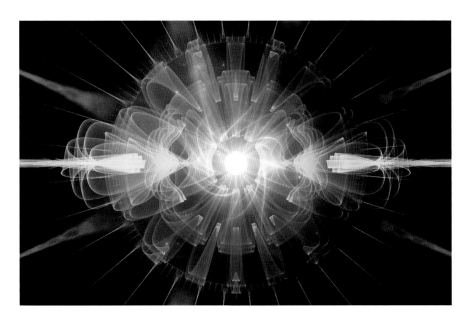

life, energy, how the universe works and how we interact with it, because essentially Source is everything.

There is no separation from Source. Separation is merely a perception, because we cannot be separated from that which we are. We are Source energy manifest in the physical, experiencing, growing and evolving on the earth plane. Our souls inhabit a body that experiences physicality, and when our physical body dies our soul continues on and chooses if it wishes to come back to learn more. I see the earth as a physical school for souls. We come, we learn lessons and we grow. We keep returning until we graduate or have learnt what we need to and accomplished everything necessary for our soul's growth.

There is a big lesson in understanding that this reality is a tool for growth. We are all here learning: by making mistakes or through hardship or trauma, but we also learn through love, gratitude and giving. This physical reality is very much like the movie *The Matrix*, in that it is partly an illusion we are able to tap into and manipulate in certain ways behind the scenes in the spiritual and energetic realms. The aim of this book is to help you expand your thinking to allow you to see the world in a different way. Once the door is open it doesn't close again, and you'll start to discover you play an important part in how your life unfolds. More importantly, once you know where you are going you can have the universe clear the way for you.

First we must make a distinction between the physical and spiritual worlds. When we die and our spirit or life force leaves our body, the physical part of ourselves decomposes and goes back to the earth. All of our elements separate: air, water, earth, fire and spirit. However, our spirit still continues and will once more return into another physical body that is a vibrational match; this is reincarnation. There are two elements at play here. One is that we have a physical body that is separate from our soul and the other is our soul, which animates the physical body. Source energy must surely then be that which animates the physical body?

There is nothing solid in the universe. Let's look at things in forms of frequency. We learned in high school that colours are just different frequency patterns of light being reflected, each with its own wave pattern. Matter is also an energy frequency: the higher the vibrational frequency the less dense the object, and the lower the frequency the denser the object will be. Think in terms of water and ice. When you cool down water to freezing temperature you slow down the speed of the molecules of water, which creates a dense structure of ice. Heat it up again and the molecules move faster, the water becomes fluid. Heat it even further and it becomes steam. The structure is relative to the amount of potential energy and the rate at which the molecules move. These are the three basic molecular structures: solid, liquid and gas.

Molecules are constantly moving because they have energy. We know that everything is made up of atoms, and that atoms are made up of mostly space … yep, space. So if molecules are mostly space, then nothing is actually solid. How come, then, you can't walk through walls if you aren't solid? Think of an egg beater: there is nothing inside them when they are turned off, but turn them on and you can't put your finger through them. Atoms are like this, in that the energy that is swirling everywhere around them, which is made up of electrons, protons, neutrons, quarks and gluons, makes a barrier around the nucleus. Essentially, you are a body of empty atoms huddling together to create form.

Everything takes up form by its vibration. In the phenomenon known as cymatics, sound or vibration can be visualised using sand or water on a metal plate attached to a speaker or sound generator. The speaker generates a specific sound frequency, which when directed at the metal plate makes the sand or water organise itself into a vibrational geometric pattern. The pattern is essentially a flat slice of a 3D geometric pattern, and depending

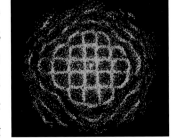

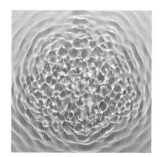

Chladni in water

Sunflower

Succulent

Ammonite

on the complexity of the sound will determine for the most part how simple or complex the pattern is.

See the geometry of the pattern? The sand huddles together and the black is where no sand congregates.

On the top left there is a Chladni image in water.

If you change the sound, the pattern will alter to something entirely different as the sand or water shifts to its next destination. The sound or vibration is what makes the atoms huddle together, which is how sound takes up form. Each sound will replicate the same pattern time and time again, as the pattern is unique to that sound.

Cymatics also gives us a glimpse into the workings of nature. Nature is very orderly and forms through geometric shapes, which can be found in practically everything. Take the sunflower, for instance, the succulent or the ammonite (pictured second, third and fourth from the top).

Every living thing on earth seems to grow to a template of its particular energy, like it has a blueprint of some sort that allows every fish to become a fish, a quartz crystal to become a quartz crystal, a baby to become a human. In order for anything to become a physical body, it first needs an energetic template that directs the cells to do what they are meant to. Or perhaps this energy template is the vibration/sound of the object?

If everything on earth and in the universe forms by its sound or vibration, where does this sound or vibration come from? Could Source be where sound originates, or is there more than one Source – one that creates a vibration which then creates a physical structure, and one that is then attracted to that vibration, which then animates the structure. This is like a yin-yang approach, a male and a female energy, or perhaps they are one and the same. Do they need to be divided into two separate entities?

It's okay if you don't fully understand this concept. The main point to take on board is that sound is what makes matter take form, that sound seems to be how Spirit can take form in the physical realm. Spirit needs a physical vibrational match in order to manifest. Does the sound then come from Spirit? Spirit/Source vibrates or makes sound in the spiritual realm, allowing energy to come down through all of the dense physical layers, which then become a solid physical structure.

The interconnectedness between the physical body and Spirit are the laws of nature. Where and why these laws exist is a mystery, but they hold the key to understanding the relationship between physicality and Source energy.

It makes me wonder if the coming together of a couple to conceive a child with the vibrations of both the egg and sperm, generate a new vibration with the creation of a new DNA. Does this then create a vibrational match to a soul that allows this soul to come into the physical body? Is the creation of a new DNA vibration what attracts the soul to it?

If everything takes up form by its vibration or sound, then surely our entire universe is one elaborate symphony that we can only see and not hear? When indigenous tribes are asked about their plant medicine knowledge and how they learnt what each herb or plant is for, their response is that plants have their own unique song or sound. If you communicate with the plant it might teach you its song, so you may better understand it and be able to use it to help heal others. Some also say that humans have their own sound or song.

We tend to view everything as physically dense structures, but when we look closer and closer, down to a microscopic level, we find that everything is made up of atoms that are constantly vibrating, are empty and have an energy field. When atoms of like consciousness come together through the law of attraction, where like is attracted to like, they then take form as shape, vibrating at a rate that creates the illusion of a physical structure. This new group of harmonised atoms now expresses a particular vibration or physical form. Even the air, which is transparent, is made up of tiny atoms, just not as condensed as physical structures. Remember the three molecular structures of gas, liquids and solids. Air is a gas, so if air is full of atoms and touches everything liquid or solid, and liquid touches everything solid, then there is no separation between anything. Every single atom on earth is touching another atom. The only difference between gas, liquid and solid structures is merely the rate at which the atoms are moving and their potential energy.

You can start to imagine that we are walking in a sea of energy. We are in a state of constant flow; nothing is solid, and we are all fluid. If you can then push your thinking out further, you can begin to imagine how you would then be able to interact with other energies around you, for they are also the same.

Why is it important to understand about matter taking form through vibration?

◊ Your thoughts and feelings are also vibrations, which is how manifesting works. Through the law of attraction you attract that which you are putting out, so it is vitally important to have your beliefs and thoughts in alignment. For example, if you want to attract money but believe you don't deserve it, only other people can achieve it or that once you have it it won't be sustainable or you'll somehow lose it means that what you want to manifest is not in alignment with your belief or what you are putting out. This is why manifesting fails time and time again – you need to believe that it is achievable.

◊ If Source is everything then nature and its beings are also Source, so you can learn about yourself by observing nature. What you do yourself you do to others; what you do to nature you do to yourself. Connecting to nature is thus vitally important. When you connect to nature you connect to Source, to yourself and to the all that is, and that is where the magic happens – you become in sync with the universe and understand how this life works and what it is here to teach you. Then you are able to navigate your life better, apparent coincidences occur and you align yourself with your true purpose.

If I am Source and I am connected to Source, then why must I learn to connect to Source? One of the reasons why we have created an illusion of separation from Source is due to the limits of our five senses. These senses help you to see, feel and interact with the physical world, but also confine your perception to only what it can see, hear and touch. We know there are other colours on the light spectrum that the human eye cannot see, such as infrared and ultraviolet rays. We know our ears cannot perceive all of the sounds around us, which is evidenced by dogs hearing sounds the human ear cannot pick up. If the human senses could relay back to you exactly how the world looks you would live in a completely different reality. You see your physical body with a definitive outline, you can feel the edges with your hands, so why would you perceive it otherwise? When you learn to use your other senses the world will open up to a whole new meaning.

We know that animals have incredible perception and understanding of the workings of nature, seeking out what they need without conscious thought. They are able to do this because they use their instincts. Do we have the same instincts? Of course we do: we are animals on earth and a part of nature; we are not separate from it. The earth is not just a platform for humans to live on; we are part of it and its ecosystem just as is every other living being on this planet.

Unfortunately, we have lost a lot of our instinctiveness through modernisation, religion and persecution. There was a time when humankind lived in harmony with nature, and happily many indigenous people still do and we are thankful that these people and their knowledge still exist today. People around the world at different times understood this connection, and many are now searching to find their way back. They feel the call, and their instincts are kicking back in.

This chapter contains concepts that may be difficult to follow or understand, but over the following chapters I'll shed light on them and how they mesh with crystal grids and manifesting. Once you are aligned and understand your connection to everything you will understand that you are a key player in how your entire life manifests. It all starts to make perfect sense when everything that happens to you is actually steering you to where you are meant to be. Working with nature and all of its gifts such as crystals and herbs is a powerful way to ask for help from the spirit realm. We have many allies in the different realms only too happy to help us if we truly wish to change and evolve.

I urge you to follow the exercises and meditations throughout the book. It is through experiencing first-hand that you will understand most. Do the practices and write them in a journal or notebook to make it special. This has been invaluable for me. Sometimes you will find that when you are writing down your experiences the real meaning comes to light. You can also look back at what you've written, which although it might not have made sense at the time will show you what has come to be upon reading it a few months later . It is only when you look back at where you were that you will understand how far you have come. You also forget a lot of the things you've done over the years. It is due to me documenting my journeys that I am able to share some of them with you in this book.

Remember that the more focused and present you are with setting your intentions the more energy will flow towards them, so something as small as the ritual of writing in your journal can have profound effects. Do not underestimate the power of small practices.

It is important to comprehend the many ways you can interact and communicate with different energies. To understand this, you must also know there are many ways of communicating in this world. Our limited human views only think of verbal communication as a language, so how, for instance, do plants communicate to us? How do we obtain messages from those who have passed over? The next chapter discusses how to break down some of the barriers to your perceived separation from Source.

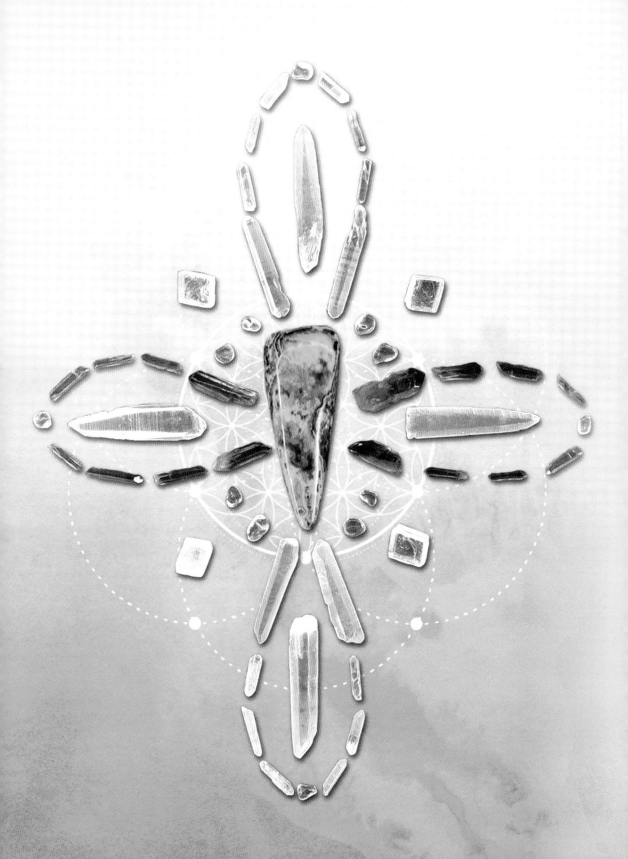

CHAPTER 2

THE LANGUAGE OF SPIRIT

Those with pets will surely know that when you are upset your pet may come to comfort you. You don't have to say anything; they just pick up on your feelings and know you need them. They can read and understand energy, and you also have this ability. First you must understand the different ways Spirit can communicate with you or how to sense the different energies beyond the five physical senses.

SPIRIT COMMUNICATION

Spirit is the term I use to describe energy, the universe, guides, ghosts, nature spirits and so on. Because I believe everything is energy just in varying degrees, it's all really one and the same.

How does Spirit communicate? I used to think you would get some sort of really obvious sign, such as seeing a ghost, observing something move by itself or hearing something unusual. It took me ages and it was while I was at a workshop that I discovered Spirit communicates very subtly. Think of the density of air compared to the density of water: it's so much harder to run through water. The same is true for Spirit trying to communicate with your

human 'dense' reality, so when their communication comes through it is like a whisper. If you are a quiet, sensitive person it might be easier to recognise, only because you spend more time in silence. However, if you are a louder and constantly on the go, you may not as easily pick up on it.

There are many ways you may receive information from Spirit. You may get images or words in your mind, along with feelings and various odours. You may actually see with your eyes or feel sensations on your skin, or just have a knowing of things. I get images, words and sensations as well as very strong intuition. I can distinguish when a particular guide is confirming something important for me because I get shivers down my right side. When something is real and there are guides confirming it, I get shivers on both the left and the right at the same time. Sometimes I just get a deep knowing where I don't even question whether it is true or not because I know it is true. Each one is a different feeling, and I have come to know which is which. It is very subtle, and it takes time and trust in yourself to understand. Everyone is different, so you need to find out what your sense is for yourself. The more you trust in this process the stronger the connection you will create. Sometimes I am overwhelmed by the amount of information or ideas I receive. I know I pick up a lot from around me, so you need to also know when to ground and protect yourself. As these are the most important things you can ever do if you wish to grow spiritually they are covered in more detail later in the book.

THE CLAIRS

Another way that you can sense energy or communicate with the other realms is through the use of your clair senses. There are numerous clair senses; the main ones are outlined below.

Clairvoyance (clear seeing). One of the most common of the clair senses, this is the ability to see images in your mind's eye about people, the past, the present and so on. You might see images both when you close your eyes and when they are open, similar to how you daydream about things. Being clairvoyant means having the ability to use your third eye chakra of insight. This chakra is in close proximity to your crown chakra, which is your ability to work with universal energy and higher beings. Thus the third eye might be seen as your internal TV screen, where higher energies are projecting their information for you to see.

Clairaudience (clear hearing). This is the ability to hear extrasensory sounds. Some people claim to be able to hear voices that speak to them; others hear noises, music or just words.

Clairsentience (clear feeling). The ability to know about emotions, thoughts or illnesses within other people just by feeling the vibration of them is another common sense people can develop. Clairsentience is when you can feel that someone is unhappy even if they claim they are fine.

Claircognisance (clear knowing). Also common, this is the ability to have knowledge with no explanation of how you know it. It can come in the form of precognition of events that may be about to occur or about events that may have occurred in the past. With this one, I usually find there is a strong connection with a knowing that what you know is also true. There generally is no doubt about what you sense could be wrong.

Clairsalience (clear smelling). Some people smell things that aren't there in the physical realm, such as smelling cigarette smoke when they sense a person who used to smoke who has passed over. It could also be the smell of the perfume of someone who is not physically there.

Clairgustance (clear tasting). Some people can taste things that remind them of a particular person or place. If you are reading for someone, you might get a taste in your mouth only they will know the significance of. It is always important to let them know what you are sensing as it might be the piece of the puzzle that brings everything together.

I can't emphasise enough how important it is to trust in what you receive even if it doesn't make sense to you at the time. You will gain a better understanding of how to decipher your messages the more you practise. Then, the more you trust in the process the easier it will become and the more confidence you will have with understanding the messages. If, for example, an image pops into your head, take note of it even if you don't understand the relevance. Try to recognise the times when things seem out of the blue or coincidental.

Always trust what you sense even if you think it's silly. The more you trust the more you will be able to decipher the messages. Many times I have read oracle cards for people and not wanted to tell them things I thought seemed ridiculous, yet when I did tell them they were ecstatic as it meant something very relevant to them. It has taught me not to filter what I receive to save embarrassment. It might be just the one thing they needed to hear, but if it doesn't mean anything to them you haven't really lost anything. Be brave.

It is also very easy to doubt yourself at first and this is okay. The messages can be so subtle at times, which is another reason to learn to slow down, centre yourself and be quiet enough to listen with your senses. You'll very rarely get messages if you are filling up every gap of silence.

INTUITION

Intuition is a huge part of working spiritually. I personally believe intuition is your soul speaking, and you can ask your soul questions if you know how to. Your soul knows what it is here for, so why not ask it? Your intuition is like your soul compass: keep following the direction of your compass and it will keep you on your path. Intuition is widely used by animals and is what we need to rely on to make proper decisions. It is also a big key when creating crystal grids. We are instinctively making our own medicine, and when you trust your gut you can't go wrong.

When I first decided to write this book I thought it was going to be about me showing people how to remember their soul; I was going to call it *Remembering Me*. It all came about after experiencing something amazing. After completing many shaman exercises, I finally came to the ritual or journey for discovering my shaman name. Journeying is similar to a guided meditation, but in shamanic practices it is about taking your consciousness to another realm to gain insight. It was the single most defining point in my life and something I have kept to myself, but I am willing to share it in these pages if it will inspire others.

When I began my journey I found myself underground in a cave and was placed on a large megalithic-type stone table. I was naked and the crone faery, a character that is now in one of my recent paintings, flittered around and took a knife and cut my skin open from head to toe. Out of my skin, a body of light rose up. I found myself in the middle world in a forest clearing with the same stone table, which I was again placed on. A massive tree that I knew to be the green man did the same to me as the faery crone. He sliced me open and my light body rose out of my skin.

I found myself in the stars, the upper world, with a star being, and she welcomed me with the words: 'Welcome, Shining One.' I asked her what my shaman name was. She replied: 'I cannot tell you this; you need to remember for yourself.' I then found myself in front of a stone door in the middle of space and again I asked what my shaman name was. I waited and waited, and then the name 'Peacewalker' came to me. I heard it over and over again. The star being said: 'You are Peacewalker, you are a light in the darkness, a beacon of hope.'

Tears were streaming down my face. I felt tears of joy, because I was fully remembering who I am. I understood at that time what and who I was, and what I was here to do. I also realised that I am still a young soul in comparison to the star being that was before me. The feeling of remembrance was something that words cannot do justice to. It certainly wasn't something I had made up, and it was the most amazing experience I have ever had in this lifetime. I thought if I could show people how to also remember who they were so they could experience this for themselves, it would give so many people hope and direction in their lives. It could show them how confined they are by their perceived reality.

I know that so many times in my life I wanted to give up and check out. I lived in a state of depression for a very long time just hoping there was more to life, but no matter how hard I tried I just couldn't make it better. I pushed myself through each day, sometimes through every minute. I lived to exist, and the thought of just existing for however many years of life I had left in me made me even more depressed.

For me to have felt like this, I knew that many others out there were also feeling this sadness and frustration. I lost a close friend to suicide, and it impacted my life for so many years afterwards that I couldn't imagine causing that pain to those who loved me. I did, however, fully understand what drives people to commit suicide. It is such a shame to see beautiful souls depart the earth but, at the same time, if you believe in reincarnation or that the body is just a vehicle for your soul to incarnate into and experience being human, then you can also understand these souls have just gone through a transition. It took me a long time to really understand the gravity of this, but now I am at a point where I know my friend is still close by. I sense him at times, and it truly is a beautiful experience knowing he is there. Who knows: one day we might end up being friends again in another lifetime and he will stick around longer next time.

What I've experienced has given me the extra motivation to make a difference in the world. I want to use the time I have left on earth to help others find their happiness. I want to learn as much as I can and reach as many people who care to listen. We are not meant to come here to live with sadness; this is just a sign of being disconnected. We are here to experience happiness, love and fulfilment. We need to help one another and live in harmony with every living being on the planet. It's time to find out what brings you joy and make your heart sing – and it starts with you! Looking inside and asking yourself what makes you happy. When you start listening to what your soul has to say by following your gut feelings and asking yourself the right questions, you will inevitably start walking on the path you originally laid out for yourself.

You may have heard different sources say things such as 'Let your intuition guide you' or 'Use your feelings as your inner compass'. I'm sure at one point in your life you have felt when something was not right but couldn't put your finger on it. This is your intuition. *Trust it*. Whenever you have a decision to make where logic or obligation will have you picking one way and your gut says the other; *always* trust your gut. Some decisions in your life will need to be based in logic, but you should keep in mind that your intuition is just as important in your decision-making. Sometimes you need to take that leap of faith and trust in yourself and the process. Great rewards come for those who trust in themselves.

Your soul communicates with you through your intuition, just like your body communicates with you through illness and dis-ease. In a similar way, Spirit communicates with you through the clairs. The more you start to understand the many forms of communication the more you will start to realign with your oneness and realise there is no separation. Intuition also comes into play in further chapters as we get real on what we want to manifest and gauge whether it is in alignment with our beliefs or life path.

MEDITATION: CONNECTING TO SOURCE

I find meditating invaluable for connecting to Source and getting in touch with your soul. The more you practise the more you will start to enjoy what you can learn from it. I absolutely have to go into meditation or journeying with a purpose. I find that when I record meditations to help me visualise, I get very clear and precise images and direction. Don't be concerned if you can't visualise anything. Many people find it challenging, but remember that you might use another sense. You may feel the meditation or sense other things, and that's totally normal. The main things to remember are:

◊　Don't try to force yourself to see something. Let it flow or you will become anxious, and this will raise your heart rate and breathing, which is the opposite of what you want to be doing.

◊　Do not discredit anything you see or feel. The first thing that pops into your mind is always something to pay attention to. And don't worry if you think you are making it up, as sometimes we do that to get started. Over time you will be able to distinguish between what is you making something up and Spirit communicating with you.

People experience different things depending on what they are most attuned to. Some people will see things, while other people will hear, feel, smell or just sense. Find what resonates with you most and work on refining that. I see images and sense words. I don't actually hear the words, but it's like a full sentence appears in my head and I don't need to read it but just know it and understand. It's as though time is irrelevant.

Before I do any meditating I do the tree of life exercise to ground myself. This is an important step before any meditation or journey, so please ensure you practise it each and every time. Consider bookmarking this page as we will be referring to it throughout the book.

I do this standing to feel as much like a tree as possible. You may have your own way of doing it, so use whatever feels comfortable for you. The tree of life exercise is an extremely valuable part of any spiritual undertaking that creates your connection to earth and to the above energies. You should draw your energy from it, just as the tree draws its energy through its roots and leaves. To ground and connect:

◊ Stand comfortably with your feet shoulder width apart and unlock your knees. You can also do this lying down or sitting up in a seat. Find your centre and breathe out all of your tension.

◊ If you are standing, rock back and forth on your feet a little to find a good position so that your balance becomes distributed evenly over your feet. You will feel any areas of tension that you need to let go of.

◊ Close your eyes and take a few deep breaths to relax and focus. Picture roots growing out of your feet and tailbone and into the earth. Send the roots down through the earth. See them pushing through all the layers of the earth.

◊ Picture a big white ball of energy in the centre of the earth. Connect your roots to the ball of light. Picture the light from this ball moving up through your roots, like a tree drawing up water and nutrients from the soil. Draw this light up through the soles of your feet and tailbone. Draw the light up through your body to your heart. It may be easier to draw the energy up on every in breath to create a good rhythm.

◊ See the light go down to your fingertips and back to your heart. See the light go up through the centre of your head. See it extending out through branches sprouted from your head, shoulders and arms. Lift your arms to also draw the power up and to feel and become the tree. Send the energy out through the ends of the branches and out through the leaves into the sky. Watch it extend up through the layers of the atmosphere into space, and reach up to touch the sun or moon (depending on the time of day).

◊   Feel the sun or moonlight on your face as you draw down its white light through your head, and trace the way back that the earth light came through you. Down through your head, to your heart, to your fingertips and back to your heart, down through your body, out through your feet and through the roots, and connect with the ball of white light in the centre of the earth.

◊   Now that you have connected like the tree of life, it is important to shield yourself. This will help deflect any negative energies but will also contain the energy you now have flowing through you.

◊   You can picture a big white or gold bubble in front of you that you step into, or maybe a shield pops up all around you. I picture three impenetrable light shields around me, but just go with whatever feels right for you. Fill your shield full of white light and know you are protected.

Below is a meditation I wrote that I recommend you record in your own voice to replay. I use voice notes on my phone to record mine. If you choose to record your own, remember to keep your voice very calm, monotone and slow. Take pauses to allow yourself to go deeper into the meditation. Switch your phone to airplane mode if you are using it to replay the meditation. Make sure you won't be interrupted by anything. Drink a glass of water, get into loose clothing and find somewhere really comfy to sit or lie down.

Take three deep breaths, and with each exhalation feel the tension drain away from you. Focus your attention on your consciousness. You will most likely feel this in your head, but you might feel it in your heart or possibly your whole body. Push your consciousness out like a bright white bubble so it encompasses your body. Every time you exhale, you need to push this bubble of consciousness out further to encompass the room you are in … then your house … then your property …now your suburb. Keep pushing it out to your state … your country … right out until your consciousness bubble reaches right around the earth. Push it out like a starburst out into the universe and feel yourself connected to everything.

Sit in this feeling and know you are connected to every living thing on earth. What can you feel? Can you sense any animal close by or feel the presence of a tree or a bird flying in the air? Can you see a grid connecting everything? Can you hear anything or smell something familiar? Push your senses out as far as you can. Do you have any emotions coming up? Do you feel happy or calm? Sit in this moment for a while and observe with all your senses. (I let the recording keep playing until two minutes is up and return to the meditation.)

When you feel it is time to return, bring your attention back to your consciousness. Pull it back to the earth. Feel it shrink down to your country … to your state … your suburb … your property … your house … back into your room. Feel it now around your body. Pull it back within your body. Sit here briefly while you feel yourself calibrate back into your physical body. Feel your hands and feet and give them a little wiggle to remind yourself where you are. Slowly open your eyes when you can and bring your attention back to where you are.

Drink another glass of water and write your experience in your journal. Don't try and decipher what you have seen or felt; just write it as descriptively as possible. Sometimes when you describe how you see it, it will become more apparent to you.

If you didn't get much from your meditation the first time, try it again and again. The more you make time to do the practice the more you will receive from it. I used to do it on the train to work sometimes. Yes, I was so intent on changing my life I would manifest the hell out of it wherever I could. I would use the time on the train to meditate on my perfect day, envisioning myself waking up next to my partner, going to the kitchen to make breakfast, waving goodbye to him with his children as he went to work and took them to school. I would head to my home office, where I would happily create all day, and then welcome my partner home at night. We would enjoy a candlelit dinner and a glass of red wine in our lounge room overlooking the beautiful tree-lined horizon.

Little did I understand how powerful this practice would be until I moved into my now home with my now partner in a house that has exactly the same layout of my vision. The carport is in the same place, the driveway is shaped the same, the bedrooms are exactly where I saw them, the kitchen and the tree-lined horizon are the same; everything is exactly how I envisaged it. Admittedly it took about five years to manifest, but it was because I had to strip away the many layers of me that stood in the way of that dream.

You need to be a vibrational match with what you wish to attract. That's where the hard work is, but if you are determined to live the life you envisage for yourself then it's the most rewarding thing you could ever give yourself in this lifetime. I'm still in awe about how it has played out, but it has given me the motivation to create the next chapter of my life.

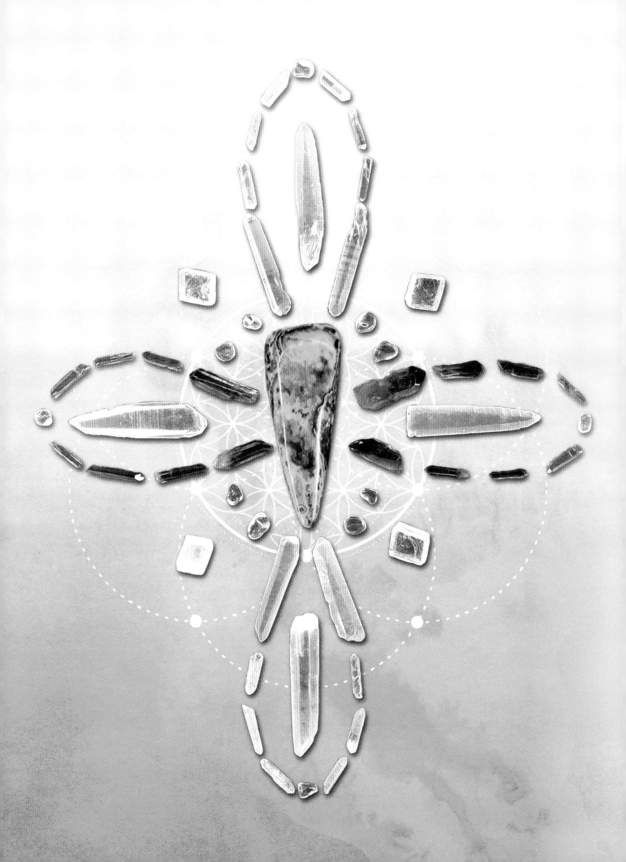

CHAPTER 3

WHAT ARE CRYSTAL GRIDS?

A crystal grid is the placement of crystals usually in some form of geometric pattern, with a main crystal in the centre and smaller crystals arranged around it. They are used to help manifest a desired intention, so essentially it becomes a physical manifestation of your intention.

Crystal grids and stone formations dating back hundreds of years can be found all around the world. For some reason humankind has been compelled to create all manner of geometric designs, from Neolithic sites such as Stonehenge to Native American medicine circles. The workings of them may never be fully understood, but we are drawn to them nonetheless. Could this pull be our intuition guiding us to our own medicine? Are we communicating with other realms intuitively by creating our own energy frequencies?

The ritual of creating a crystal grid has many facets. Placing a bunch of crystals in a pretty pattern and just expecting it to help you manifest what you want is not going to be effective. Creating a crystal grid by thoroughly understanding what you want to manifest, using key elements you need for your specific issue created under ritual with intent and clear focus, are the keys to effective crystal grids. Rituals are a means to shift your consciousness into an altered state so that you can solely focus on your

Example of a simple crystal grid using celestite as the centre stone surrounded by quartz and calcite.

intent. It is this focused intent that is imperative to manifesting: where thought goes, energy flows.

Crystal grids can be basic or incredibly complex, depending entirely on how you want to create one. I like to keep them fairly simple by using no more than five or six different-coloured stones, as this is what resonates with me. If you feel inclined to use more, then follow your intuition. My reasoning behind using less stones comes from my background in herbal medicine, and it is the same with flower essence therapy. Using too many herbs or flowers in a mix can be confusing and can overload the body and give it too much to do. You can use herbs or flowers that have similar actions together to boost the potency, and this is what I do with crystals.

HOW CRYSTAL GRIDS WORK

Be as open as possible to the following as you can. Allowing other possibilities to exist will make you aware of realities other than your own. I am still learning and acquiring knowledge to help me understand the reality of other worlds that co-exist within my own. The more I allow my mind to be free of learned beliefs or limits, the more is being revealed to me.

'Open your mind to see the beauty of something unnoticed.'
– NICOLA MCINTOSH

Crystal grids allow you to tap into and work with Source energy, because Source energy is in everything. It's in the crystals you use, and it is in you when you call on your spirit helpers and guides to be with you when creating your grid; they are also Source. The energetic patterns you create with the placement of your crystals will create more frequencies and draw more Source energy to your grid.

Then the law of attraction will come into play. When you are manifesting things into your life you manifest more of what you *are*. If you are emanating love you will draw more love to yourself. If you are emanating anger you will draw more situations that make you angry.

It is vitally important to understand exactly what you want to manifest and what you need to acquire to create a grid that is a vibrational match to your intent. For instance, if you want to draw more love into your life you would look at the chakra involved with working with love, the heart chakra. You would then source green or pink crystals, stones or elements that work with the heart chakra to place in your grid. You would also look at what geometric grid pattern would be the most appropriate to place your crystals on, then find an intent statement that is aligned in the present tense. Why the present tense? Because you wish to attract more of what you are and not what you would like in the future, or you would then be manifesting something that was always in the future.

Each crystal has its own particular frequency or vibration. Quartz in particular has some very special properties, which is why you will find most of my grids contain mainly quartz (see Chapter 5 for more detail on crystals). Quartz is able to be programmed with your thoughts, because as we have already learned your thoughts and emotions are vibrations. Quartz also amplifies energy, so it can essentially amplify your program. Spirit can choose to work through quartz and crystals for specific purposes (this is also discussed in Chapter 5).

Just as with herbal medicine and flower essence therapy, when you put two or more crystals together they work synergistically and are sometimes more effective than just having a single crystal. You can also program the crystals in the grid for your specific purpose or intention, which will bring the vibrations of the crystals together for the same purpose and increase their unified vibration.

What happens when you put an intention out to the universe? The law of attraction brings you more of what you are sending out. If you have amplified your intention through the use of programmed crystals placed in a harmonic pattern to increase their vibration and have used quartz, which amplifies all energy that goes through it, you create an extremely powerful manifesting tool. The combination of programmed crystals is like a beacon that continues to send out your intention even when you are not thinking about it. If you continue to send it energy, therefore recharging it, it will continue to keep your intent going.

GEOMETRIC DESIGN

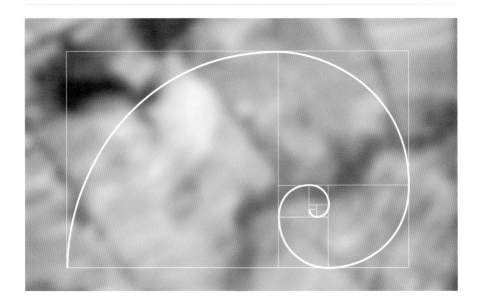

We generally create crystal grids in a geometric pattern because geometry is the architecture of the universe. As has been previously noted, the laws of nature are defined through this geometry. Each geometric shape has its own vibration, so when crystals are arranged in a geometric pattern their energy fields also overlap with the other crystals in the grid. The intersections where these energies overlap then create their own vibration. There are many types of geometric patterns that can be used with crystal grids for different purposes, which is discussed in Chapter 6.

You can also create your grids intuitively, which can be equally as important. Whatever the reason for choosing a particular geometric design for your grids, you will be instinctively tapping into a vibrational source within them.

CHAKRAS

Chakras are extremely important to consider when creating crystal grids, because when manifesting it helps to use as many aligned energies as possible. Most of the issues you are hoping to shift in your life relate back to imbalances in your chakras. When you have a good understanding of how your everyday problems relate to specific chakras, you'll be able to select the right crystals for the job with ease. You might like to carry just one stone or crystal of each chakra colour in your crystal toolkit, and that will be all you need to get started.

Using a crystal grid may give you the ability to communicate with the vast network of channels within the workings of nature and the universe. You can send your message to every corner of the earth. Using the law of attraction will enable you to have that energy come back to you with the information you need or particular circumstances to ensure you receive what you are asking for. This is why it is extremely important to know what you want to manifest.

In the bigger scheme of things you don't really need any tools at all as you can tap into Source energy to manifest at any time through practices such as meditation, but crystal grids do help you to focus and magnify your intent. The actual ritual of simply creating a grid allows you to get into the right mindset for focusing your intent. Over time and with practice, you will strengthen your ability to understand the source you are connected to, the source that you are and will be able to communicate with freely.

THE IMPORTANCE OF RITUAL

To reiterate, it is pointless just throwing some coloured crystals in a pretty pattern and expecting it to perform. Creating crystal grids in ritual is an extremely important step. Doing anything in ritual, doesn't necessarily mean a donning your cape and getting out your cauldron type of ritual, which is of course one way to do it. A ritual is anything you do with purpose and intent and can be whatever you decide to make it; if you have a cauldron and a cape, that's great! If you don't and that's not you, find what sits right with you. Just know that when you call on Spirit to help you and you are in the present, focusing on your intention, that is ritual, that is when all the spiritual energies are called together in order for you to let them know your intent.

Prayer is also a ritual. There is great power in calling on the help of Spirit and letting whatever it may be know you need help. We all have spirit guides that help us in life; they are always there, but they aren't watching us intently

24 hours a day for seven days a week. When you need them you need to get their attention, which is why you call them in or ask them for their help. When you do anything in ritual and call in all the spirit helpers, whether that be your guides, angels, crystal spirits or animal totems, it's like calling a big board meeting and letting everyone know at once exactly what your plan is, getting everyone on the same page and then having them go off and take care of their side of the plan.

WHAT CRYSTAL GRIDS ARE USED FOR

Essentially, crystal grids are used to either bring energy into your space or to send intent out into the environment. The limits are endless when it comes to the use of crystal grids, but here are some examples:

◊ **Manifestation:** to help you manifest a specific desire, such as a job, abundance, love or help with a project.

◊ **Property:** you can grid an entire property for protection or just your house or maybe just a room. You can make a grid to create a specific atmosphere in a room, to make it full of love, for instance. You can grid your bedroom to help you sleep at night.

◊ **Health:** you may be suffering from a specific health issue you would like help with. This can also apply for someone other than yourself who may need this healing.

◊ **Distance healing:** because you can direct energy anywhere, you can use grids to send healing to others over distance.

◊ **Crystal essences:** these can be created when you have your grid set up and can be taken internally for extra healing or insight. They hold the resonance of your crystal grid.

◊ **Divination:** just like my crystal grid oracle, you can intuitively create a grid and then take the time to understand what you have created and why you might need it at this time.

◊ **Meditation:** crystal grids are a great tool to aid meditation. It could be a centre grid for a group meditation or a grid on your altar, or you might like to create a large grid that you can sit or lie in to help you meditate or for healing.

◊ **Healing the earth:** Wouldn't it be awesome if we all created grids to help heal the earth and raise the vibration of the planet?

You might be thinking: 'Really, can crystal grids do that much?' If you follow the steps, then yes, they can. Remember it is more about *you* and what you put into it that will make the difference. You don't have to make an elaborate grid. You have to be extremely mindful of your impact on the earth, which includes the efficacy and sustainability of crystals in the marketplace. Don't feel you need to have a large array of crystals to choose from. If you can purchase your crystals from ethical sources, please do so. If you can join a fossicking club and fossick for quartz crystals yourself even better, or why not support your local lapidary club when they have open days?

We live in an age that is consumed by greed, and unfortunately the crystal industry is no exception. Many crystal dealers are doing disastrous things to the environment and creating poor conditions for their workers. Crystals and stones are being pulled out of the earth at an ever-increasing rate each day, and prices are going up. If this doesn't sit right with you, go to a place in nature or find a riverbed and collect some river stones or pebbles. You don't have to create a crystal grid with just crystals; stones of any sort are from Source energy and still have Spirit.

It is more about intent and connection than anything else. You can create grids from flowers, leaves, bark and found objects, even jewellery. Please don't feel constrained by not having crystals or being able to acquire what you want. I will show you how to substitute any crystal you don't have but feel you need. The time now calls for learning how to connect to the energies of the crystals, and if you feel confident you can do this without them or are willing to learn how to then you are already a step ahead.

There are three parts to crystal grids:

◊ **Intent:** it's about fine-tuning your intention and really discovering what you truly want to manifest; you cannot manifest something if you do not know what you want. Manifesting is about brainstorming and getting real about what you truly desire. It's about defining what success for you looks like and working towards that goal.

◊ **Being open to receive:** once your crystal grid has been created, you must be open to receive the energy, guidance and healing it will provide you. This is where you need to understand your way in perceiving energy, that is, the clair senses, but also you need to take notice of any coincidences that happen or events and people who might be messengers.

◊ **Taking action:** there's no point in going to all this trouble of wanting to manifest something if you are not prepared to take the action you need to bring it to fruition. With any spiritual work, it's also about doing the physical work yourself. Depending on what you wish to manifest, this could mean an entire overhaul of your life in order for you to become aligned and be a vibrational match to what you want to manifest. For example, if you want to become an international singer but are incredibly shy or introverted, in order for you to manifest your desire you might have to strip away your social awkwardness first in order for you to become a vibrational match for the outcome you have chosen. Obviously some things you wish to manifest might not require much from you, but be prepared for the potential shifts ahead.

You should by now be able to understand that crystal grids, as with any form of medicine, require a bit of thought. This is not to say you can't quickly create something, but my point is you will get out what you put in. When you take a logical and systematic approach to creating a grid for a specific purpose you draw together in one place many similar energies to hear what you need. The first stop is learning a simple approach to understanding chakras, because once you learn these well the rest will fall easily into place.

'Once you make a decision,
the universe conspires
to make it happen.'

— RALPH WALDO EMERSON

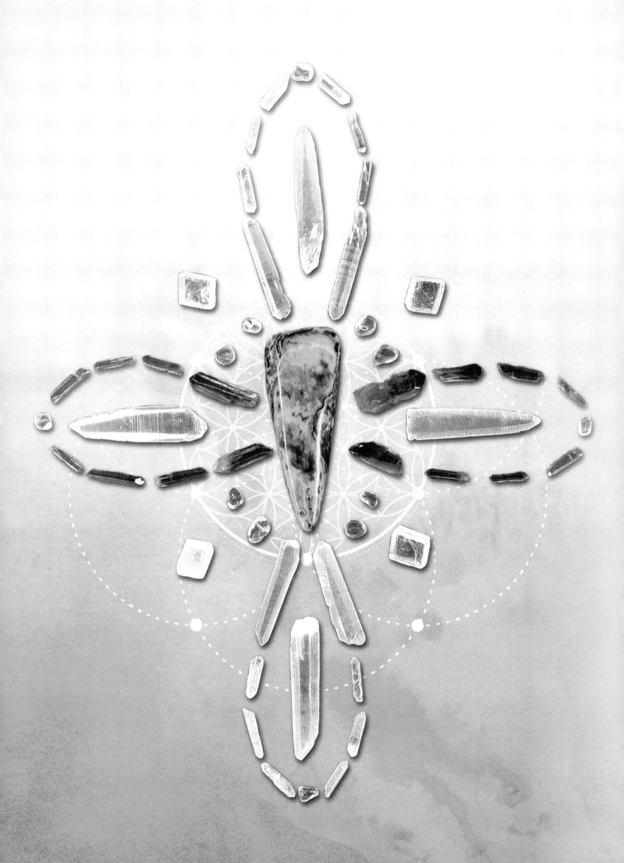

CHAPTER 4

—

CHAKRAS

The chakras are believed to have come from ancient Indian Sanskrit texts; chakra in Sanskrit means 'wheel'. Chakras are thought to be spinning wheels of energy within the body that help integrate subtle energies down to a physical level. Each chakra is associated with a colour, nerve plexus and an endocrine organ, so if you do healing on your chakras through the use of crystals, colour, yoga or meditation it will filter down to the corresponding physical centre.

Each chakra develops sequentially as we grow, and each holds its own lessons. There are seven main chakras that most people identify with; however, some traditions believe there are five chakras, while others think nine or 12. For the purpose of this book we will stick to the seven main chakras. If you feel inclined to work with other chakra systems, by all means do; always trust your intuition. There are also many smaller chakras within the body, so once you have an understanding of the main ones you might want to continue your journey into these. You may already be able to feel the ones you have in the palms of your hands. Energy workers generally feel a warmth in these centres when doing reiki or healings.

CROWN CHAKRA — UNIVERSAL TRUTH / HIGHER SELF

THIRD EYE CHAKRA — INSIGHT / CLAIRVOYANCE

THROAT CHAKRA — EXPRESSION / COMMUNICATION

HEART CHAKRA — LOVE / NATURE

SOLAR PLEXUS CHAKRA — SELF-ESTEEM / WISDOM

SACRAL CHAKRA — SEXUALITY / CREATIVITY

ROOT CHAKRA — FAMILY / SURVIVAL

CHAKRA SYSTEM

This is what can happen if your chakra is out of balance; let's take the throat chakra as an example. If you hold back from telling someone something it means you are holding energy back in the throat location. This can cause an imbalance in the chakra that filters down to the physical body, giving you a cough, lump in the throat or sore throat. You can work on removing the blockage of energy from the throat via use of a particular blue stone placed on your chakra or meditating on the throat chakra, or you could just voice what you need to say. On the other hand, you may have an overactive throat chakra that gives rise to you over-talking or also having a sore throat or cough.

Underactivity is a deficiency and overactivity is an excess; either way you look at it, it is an imbalance that needs to be balanced. If energy isn't flowing where it should it will go elsewhere or bank up until it finds an escape route.

Keep in mind that an energy imbalance can come from a chakra down to the physical body or vice versa. You can work on the body using chakra therapy or work from the inside out with herbal medicine or conventional medicine to create a change.

CHAKRAS AND CRYSTAL GRIDS

The purpose of this book is to help you manifest change within your life. The chakras are a way in which you can understand your life lessons and learn from your experiences, which essentially allows you to evolve to a higher consciousness as you work from the base chakra up. Practically any situation or anything you wish to manifest can be related back to a specific chakra. For instance, if you wish to find love you might want to work with your heart chakra; however, if you are closed off to love due to trauma that happened to you as a child it might benefit you to work with your base or sacral chakras, which relate to family, stability and relationships.

If you understand how your chakras work and can determine where an issue is coming from you can use the colour of your grid and specific stones to work on that particular chakra. This is like having an extra layer added to your grid to enhance your intention. You will then receive the perfect information, energy or healing needed to help you work on yourself, which will allow you to become a vibrational match to what you want to manifest. If you are not aligned it may be the reason a crystal grid you made in the past didn't work. Manifestation is all about aligning yourself to what you are asking for, not just asking and expecting to get what you asked for.

CHAKRA ASSOCIATIONS

Starting with the base chakra and working up to the crown chakra, you learn the energies of each chakra as you grow and can see the natural progression of lessons as you go through each one. The chakras seem to be vital energy centres that are commonly overlooked, but they offer a wealth of information to anyone who studies them. You are made up of energy, and the more you understand the interplay between everything the more you will ultimately learn about yourself and your impact on the world.

BASE CHAKRA: EARTH

The base chakra is associated with your connection to the element of earth, and to family, physical energy, survival, courage, stability, material issues, passion and grounding.

This is the first chakra lesson about family, stability, survival and taking action. Survival is a key message here, along with stability. It is your first chakra lesson when you are born, you rely on your family and your mother and father to provide all of the basics for survival as you are too young to do this yourself. If your needs are met you don't fear you are going to die, but if your needs are not met you will start to live in fear. Your survival instincts might always be on high alert and you may feel it is a daily struggle to just get by. If you have issues to do with work or wanting to change your career it is a base chakra issue, because it relates to your survival. Also, look to the base chakra if you lack physical energy or motivation towards getting a project done.

The base chakra is like the foundation of your house: if you are solidly grounded and have good balance in this chakra, it creates stability in the chakras above it. This chakra controls your blood and circulatory system, which is also red, and is connected to your adrenal glands, which controls your fight or flight response when stressed. Your adrenals raise your heart rate, and if you are in a constant state of stress you will drain your body of energy and burn out. This is why it is key to keep up your nutrition to give your body the right building blocks and energy it needs to function and provide the rest of your body with stability.

Family or tribe is another key message here, and refers to your immediate family. If you have been abandoned or outcast in some form or have issues with your family, problems may arise in this chakra.

Passion, or your physical attraction and lust, is also part of your base chakra. Passion is a primal urge and a primitive act to ensure survival, so these feelings can be very strong.

Many people I come across today are not as grounded as they should be. We are living in a society that no longer resides in small tribal communities that help one another, and are mentally driven at an ever-increasing, unsustainable pace. This gives you little time to really be still and ground yourself, let alone recharge your body. Doing a lot of mental or spiritual work can focus your energy in the top half of your body, mainly the head, and especially if you sit at a computer all day and rarely move around. When the energy is in your head you may feel scattered, can't turn your inner chatter off at night when trying to sleep and may get headaches. In these cases grounding is particularly important, as it brings all that excess energy down and connects you back to the earth, allowing tension and stress to ground out to create balance again in your body. Eating will also ground and nourishes you, so what you put into your body is vital for this chakra.

SACRAL CHAKRA: WATER

Being of the water element, we connect the sacral chakra to emotions and to flow; it is also related to relationships, desire and pleasure. This chakra is connected to the female reproductive organs, which create life, and that is why we also associate this chakra with creativity.

You will be aware of imbalances in this chakra because they are linked to emotional over-sensitivity or dependence. It could, however, be the complete opposite, with someone who represses their feelings or sexuality remembering that each chakra has a deficient or excess state. You might also have a creative block of some sort. Keep in mind that this chakra relies on the base chakra for energy, and that the base chakra is about physicality. If you are adrenally exhausted – a base chakra issue – you might be too exhausted to create – a sacral chakra issue. Each chakra can have an effect on the next.

The sacral chakra is also linked to relationships, although moving on from the family relationships of the base chakra to friendships and partnerships, including your relationship with money. In my opinion money is linked to a few chakras. It can be a base chakra issue related to survival, but also a sacral chakra as it relates to creating money and your relationship with money.

Your relationship to money starts at a young age, especially if you keep in mind that the base chakra is the first chakra you work through and the sacral is the second. If you are born into a poverty consciousness it can be difficult to understand anything else, therefore, the cycle continues through each generation. The same can generally be said for having a lot of wealth: if you haven't had to struggle for money you won't be putting out the energy that it's hard to acquire. If you have suffered the loss of money or a business it can create issues in your sacral and base chakras, because losing a business or financial stability is a basic survival skill, hence a base chakra issue. Your relationship to money will also be affected and you'll fear you will repeat the same pattern, so when you set up your grid you might wish to use red and orange crystals or stones to work on these chakras when wanting to change your vibration around money and abundance.

SOLAR PLEXUS CHAKRA: FIRE

Your solar plexus has many functions and is related to your ego, self-esteem, intelligence and assimilation. When you think of fire you can think of either warmth and comfort or fear, as it has the ability to inspire both of these feelings in us. The solar plexus chakra is linked to your digestive organs, so how you digest and assimilate things is key here. Assimilation relates to how you eat on the run or sit and enjoy your meals. It is also the amount of information you take in on a daily basis, and with social media the amount of information you are trying to assimilate in your spare time when you could be recharging is probably having a massive impact on your body. If you live in a fear-based world you will assimilate and digest life as though everything is to be feared. When you just let the natural flow of life happen you allow your solar plexus to function normally.

The solar plexus and its fire is also related to your will, or the fire in your belly. Think of what fire does: it transforms and moves upwards, just as willpower propels us forward.

Your solar plexus is associated with intelligence; it is like a library of all the events in your life. You learn to catalogue these events as a reference point as you grow. If you have stored away inaccurate views of your life events or have been dominated by another you may have a distorted way of reacting to situations.

The solar plexus is where you will find your self-esteem and ego. Essentially, this centre is about knowing yourself and what happens to you as you grow, and generally defines how you feel about yourself. Sometimes it is easy to tell when someone has a lot of ego or is controlling as they will have an extra-large belly due to the excess energy in that area. Conversely, someone who has little self-esteem or is being dominated by someone can have a very sunken belly or poor posture, as though shrinking away from life. They don't have enough personal power to stand tall and be proud of who they are. If someone does not allow you to be yourself you will create a block in this area and will have feelings of being hard done by. When you are balanced in this chakra you will realise everyone is equal and the world does not owe you anything.

Ego, I find, only presents itself when you do not love yourself or are not confident with who you are; you create a persona that you think the world will accept. When you no longer care what others think of you you show yourself fully to the world and your ego melts away.

HEART CHAKRA: AIR

Without air, fire cannot burn. The solar plexus relies on the heart chakra and the physical body. The heart chakra is associated with your lungs, which draw in air, and your heart, which draws in blood. It thus relates to how you draw in life and create balance between your internal and external environments. It has been explained that your base chakra is your relationship with family, your sacral chakra is your relationship with partners and money and your solar plexus is your relationship to self. Your heart chakra is your relationship to the world and nature; it is how you connect to your external environment. We think of nature being green, just like the heart chakra.

The heart chakra is about love: how you love yourself and how you love others. Love is the universal energy that connects everything, the means by which you communicate with every living being. It is the fundamental driving force of the law of attraction. When you accept and love yourself you are able to accept and love others free from judgement.

From your heart centre you show compassion for others regardless of where they are in their life lessons. When you lead from a compassionate and loving heart centre you will attract exactly that experience to yourself. Your life will be full of people and situations that reflect your love and compassion back to you.

We also associate the colour pink with love. I see bright pink in auras when there is love and I see it in my own when I am feeling love. I associate the heart chakra with both pink and green, and use these stones in my grids when working with any issues associated with the heart chakra.

Being the chakra that relates to drawing in life it is also about how you receive; if you are not open to receiving it may be a heart chakra issue. You might be a very giving person, but when someone tries to give you something, whether it be a gift or even a compliment, take notice of how you react. Do you take it and say thank you, or do you shy away and say it's not necessary or you don't need it? Many times we can be closed off to receiving and not know it. Take notice of whether you shallow breathe or take nice big deep breaths. People who are caregivers can deplete their heart chakra by giving and giving and never receiving. You can give and give because you care greatly, which is not a bad thing, but you must remember to give back to yourself. You cannot pour from an empty cup.

The centre of the chakra system, the heart chakra is where the dense energy of the lower chakras meet with the high vibrational energy of the higher chakras, and also where the outer world meets the inner world. It is where you learn to integrate all the aspects of your life. As above, so below; as within, so without. Getting to the heart of the matter is about understanding all aspects of your life and how they all interrelate. Working on matters of the heart can bring you great enlightenment and peace, not only within yourself but with everyone and everything around you.

THROAT CHAKRA: ETHER

When you look at the elements of each chakra you will notice that the base chakra starts with the heavy earth element, then it works up to the fluid but still dense water element, then to fire, which becomes lighter, up to air, which is no longer a solid, and finally up to ether. As you progress upwards, this shows how the energy shifts on the scale from grounded, dense earth to the light element of ether. Ether is said to contain all of the previous four elements.

Your throat chakra is the centre for your expression and communication. Every lesson you have learned while growing up results in who you are today, and this is then expressed through your throat chakra. Expression comes in many forms, from verbal to creative, to even how you decide to dress to express your individuality. It shows you how vitally important it is to nourish a child's form of expression instead of trying to mould it to society's ways, which can lead to blocks in this area. Expressing yourself is a release of energy, so if you are forced to hold that energy in it has to go somewhere, which can eventuate in a total shutdown in communication. Excess energy can then manifest as excess in another chakra to which it is trying to escape. If you hold on to this energy for too long it may even manifest in a sore throat, a lump in the throat or other throat issues.

The lesson of this chakra is to be yourself. Voice what you need to, be who you need to be and create what you want to regardless of whether you think you are good or not. It is not about being the best at it; it is about allowing yourself to let the energy flow. You know what it's like to want to say something to someone who may have hurt you: you feel an overwhelming amount of energy that collects in your chest area or you can't stop your head from going over it all. This is the energy backing up to the chakras around your throat, and it can cause anger and illness. Remember that voicing something doesn't have to be verbal; you can express it through writing out what you want to say and then burning it. This can have the same effect, because it allows the energy to be released.

In my opinion the throat chakra is also closely linked to your solar plexus, your self-esteem chakra. If you don't feel confident expressing yourself you can then work with both of these chakras by using yellow and blue stones in your grids. Always keep in mind that many of the issues you may experience are multifaceted, so try and see how your chakras work with each other. Colour therapy is used with restoring chakras, so if you have an engagement that requires you to speak or you will need to communicate, not only can you carry blue stones with you but you can also wear blue colours.

THIRD EYE CHAKRA: LIGHT

'Third eye' is a good name for this chakra, as it is all about seeing what can't be seen. You can't see the third eye in the middle of your forehead, but this chakra allows you to sense and see in your mind's eye that which can't be seen by your physical eyes. I view the third eye as being purple, but you will often see it represented as indigo. Don't get too caught up on this; just go with whatever sits right with you and remember the key lessons of the chakra.

The third eye chakra is about *in*-sight, or the ability to look within and get in touch with your intuition, which I believe is communicating with your own soul. It is the centre where you receive clairvoyant experiences, which makes sense if this chakra is related to your insight. The third eye is also about vision. You can perceive messages from Spirit or from your intuition through images, which normally requires some sort of detachment from emotional and logical thinking. When you meditate, this essentially is what you are doing: calming down all the emotions and thinking to give yourself space to tune in to yourself.

Messages also come through your crown chakra for you to decipher through your third eye. These two chakras work hand in hand and are in close proximity to one another. When you are constantly working on spiritual activities these two chakras can operate quite energetically, which is why you need to ground your energy at all times as you can receive too much information and it can be difficult to discern what you need. This leads to being quite scattered and having far too many ideas that you feel you need to complete. These are your receiving areas, so if you feel overwhelmed by the amount of information you are receiving do something physical to ground and shift the energy from your head into the lower, denser part of your body and into the earth.

CROWN CHAKRA: THOUGHT

I feel that the crown chakra is white/clear, although you might notice in other references it is classed as violet. Go with what sits right for you. In my experience it has always been a white to clear chakra, which is why I use white and clear crystals when working with it and not violet or purple.

Your crown chakra is your connection to the universe, just like your base chakra is your connection to the earth. This is where you feel a connection to a higher power, which gives you faith in life, spiritual purpose, wisdom, peace and oneness. When you have imbalances in this chakra it is often associated with psychological disorders, headaches and confusion. Sometimes you can tend to live more on the spiritual side and withdraw from the earth plane to hide from trauma, which leads to withdrawal or being away with the fairies.

The crown is a good chakra to work with when wanting to open your mind to other possibilities and wisdom through thinking outside of the confines of everyday, limited thought. If it's answers you are seeking this is a good place to start, as well as with your third eye chakra for insight. The crown chakra is the chakra of knowing, which is related to claircognisance or clear knowing. When you experience this sensation you don't question the source, because you are tapping into Source. It is believed that this chakra is linked to Source, the all-knowing.

When you are feeling bogged down by the frustrations of physical reality, it is important to work with this chakra. It enables you to see and understand from a higher perspective: you can see the bigger picture from here. Meditation is a beautiful way to practise this. You gain enlightenment tapping into this source, where you are closer to your higher self and the knowledge that you are more than your physical body. You are closer to the remembrance of who you truly are.

When working with your higher chakras you must keep grounded. So using the dark earthy or red stones for your base chakra with your white and clear stones for this area will be very helpful.

CHAKRA MEDITATION

Discovering which chakras are in need of attention might be obvious to you now after reading about their qualities, but sometimes your issues will elude you. Meditation can help with identifying which chakras may be in need of some work, and this can be a very important exercise to help you take ownership of your own healing. I recommend you first record the meditation to play back to yourself, remembering to talk slow and monotonal and give yourself big pauses. Get your journal ready, get comfortable, have a sip of water and perform the tree of life exercise before you start.

Take three deep breaths, and with each exhalation feel the tension drain away. As you feel yourself getting more and more relaxed, bring your attention to your base chakra at the bottom of your spine. What colour do you experience there? Is it red, or is there another colour there? Is it glowing? Does it feel open or closed?

Move up to your sacral chakra under the belly button area. Can you sense which colour is here? You may see it is as orange, or there might be another colour. Can you feel or sense if it is open or closed? Do not be concerned if you can't sense this, and do not be concerned if you sense it is closed.

Move up now to your solar plexus, which is between your belly button and the middle of your chest, and again observe the colour of this chakra. Do you see or feel it to be yellow? Take note of any sensations you may be feeling as you work through each chakra. Can you sense if this chakra is open or closed?

Move up to your heart chakra, which lies between your breasts. You may sense this chakra as being green, but you may also feel pink here. Take notice of your breathing: is it shallow, or are you taking in deep breaths? Is your chest constricted or is it relaxed? Do you feel your heart chakra is open or closed?

Move up to your throat chakra, which might be your blue centre. Take note of how this centre feels: does it feel constricted in any way? Feel if this chakra is strong or weak, open or closed.

Move up to your third eye chakra, positioned around the middle of your forehead. Are you sensing the purple located in this area? Are you receiving any images or feelings here? Do you feel the energy here spinning open or being closed?

Finally, move up to your crown chakra on the top of your head. Do you experience any colour here? Is it white, or do you see or sense it as being clear? You might sense it as being violet. Can you feel the chakra as being open or closed? Do you sense or see the colour red here in your mind's eye?

I want you to imagine you are standing under a beautiful waterfall. The sun is shining and the water is cool but not cold. You feel the water move over your skin and flow through you, cleansing all your chakras and invigorating your entire body. Let the water flow and soothe you as you bask in the sun. Feel refreshed, feel energised, feel at peace. Stay in this image for a full minute. (If you are recording, just let it keep recording and time it for one minute.)

It is now time to come back. Bring your attention to your room. Feel the seat you are sitting on, and wiggle your toes and fingers. When you feel ready, open your eyes.

This is a perfect time to journal down what you experienced with each chakra; draw a diagram if it is quicker for you. Write down if you felt one chakra was stronger than the other or if one felt very weak. You may have also received images or sensations that you didn't quite understand. Write or draw these down too, as they may become more meaningful down the track.

Don't be concerned if you didn't quite get anything in your meditation. Meditating can take time to learn, but be persistent and keep trying. Don't worry if you think you are making it up, either. The more you do it the easier it will become.

CHALLENGE

After doing your chakra meditation and sensing whether a chakra is stronger or weaker, can you think of anything in your life or about yourself that directly relates back to that chakra? For example, you have a sore throat and you sensed that your throat chakra was weak. Is there something you are holding back from saying or expressing?

HOMEWORK

Take note of what your favourite and least favourite colours are. Be aware of what coloured clothing you usually like to wear or what colour crystals you tend to buy and have around you. Do you have a favourite pendant that you like to wear? If so, what colour is it? Do you avoid wearing certain colours?

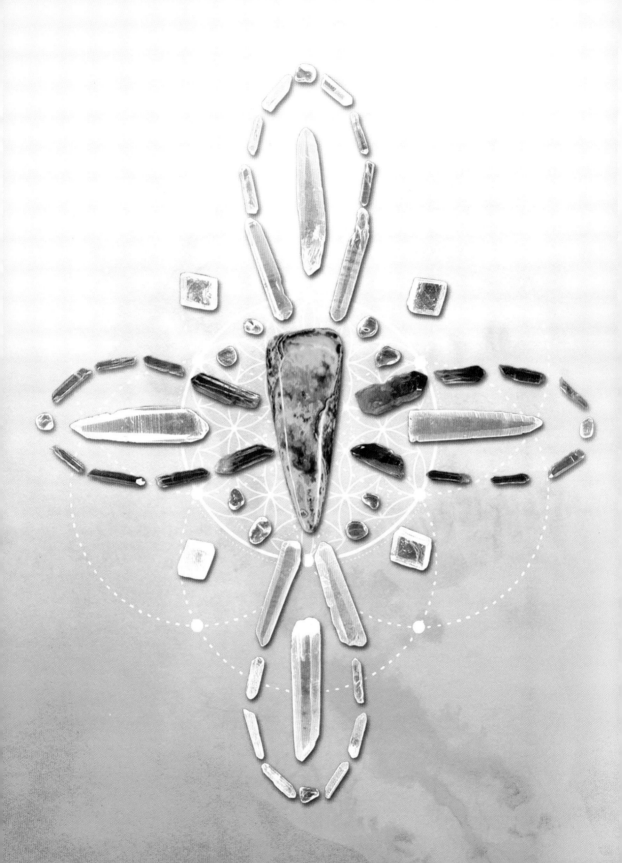

CHAPTER 5

CRYSTALS 101

Crystals have the most orderly structure in nature, and form in the most magnificent ways. We have been drawn to them for centuries, not only for their beauty but also for their metaphysical properties. There are many skeptics who doubt these properties, but for someone who has experienced what they can do there is no denying it. Even if it were true that crystals have no healing properties, just the fact that they make us feel good when we hold them is healing in itself.

The problem with crystals is that there is much conflicting information out there on exactly what they do, and it can make the crystal industry seem unbelievable. You can read a book that states a particular crystal has certain properties, only to read in another book that it has different properties. What I've come to realise is that each crystal colour corresponds to a chakra colour, so that crystal works on the issues of that chakra. Sounds simple, right? It sure is! Once you know your chakras well you can then understand what each crystal is for. For example, we know the base chakra is about family issues, stability and survival; therefore, we know that red stones work with these issues.

Why are there so many differing qualities listed for each crystal, and why are they used for certain ailments not related to the chakra colour in any way?

It is for these three reasons:

1. There is a lot of misinformation that continues to circulate and recirculate.
2. We can have certain crystal spirits that work through crystals, and they may direct you to how that particular crystal energy is to be used.
3. The doctrine of signatures is a term given to herbal medicine, in that how a plant is used may be inferred by what it looks like or where it grows. I have found this applies to crystals as well, and feel this is the way we need to go in terms of thoroughly understanding the properties of crystals. This will be explained in more detail later in the chapter.

CRYSTAL SPIRITS

Everything on this earth that is alive and grows has an energy capable of spiritual evolution. All beings come from the one Source energy, but we each have our own individual consciousness.

Behind every species of plant, tree or animal or particular crystal there is an archetypal energy that makes each group what it is. This is a tricky one to explain, but bear with me; we'll take the oak tree as an example. What does the oak tree represent, or what energy archetype embodies this tree? The archetypal energy of the oak is a symbol of strength, stability, protection, grounding, thresholds and ancient knowledge. This mass of strong energy manifests itself in the physical form of the oak tree. To apply that to crystals, quartz is a magnifier with a high vibration that aids focus and helps you connect to higher energies. The quartz crystal is the physical manifestation of that energy, which has a level of consciousness. Because you are from the same energy source, you are also able to communicate with this consciousness. It is up to you to learn its language of communication. It's not about thinking there is a little being inside there that speaks your language; it's about understanding there is another expression of Source energy that has manifested itself into the physical crystal, just as your body houses your spirit or Source energy. You are able to communicate with it because you are of the same Source; you just need to learn its language

Communicating with plants and crystals works in the same way: you have to discover the way in which you receive, that is, your clair sense, and use that to communicate. My way of receiving is through clairvoyance (vision) and claircognisance (knowing), so when I communicate with crystals or plant energy I see imagery and I get understanding or knowing. Both normally come together, so I understand what I'm seeing at the same time. I can communicate during meditative states or I do shamanic journeying. Both work equally well; however, I find that journeying allows me to go deeper and get more substantial knowledge and understanding.

Another truth I believe is that other beings can communicate to us through the crystals. Beings can enter certain crystals with the same archetypal energy to enhance our lessons. You may get a strong affinity for a specific crystal, which may be because a guide of yours can make itself known to you more easily through the use of the crystal.

This is similar to what Ted Andrews stated in his book *Animal-speak* (Llewellyn Publications, 2002): '... the animal has a spirit of its own, but sometimes a being will use the animal to communicate messages of the world to humans.' This is how a medium works: Spirit can communicate through the use of a medium, so it's not really that much of a stretch of the imagination.

Edmund Harold goes further in his book *Crystal Healing* (Viking, 1992), explaining that a quartz crystal being is 'unaware of "outer" experiences. It is caught up within its crystalline world. When you choose to work with the crystal and dedicate it to Universal Purpose, it will desire to be a part of that "outer" world. Like a chick trying to break free from its shell, its electromagnetic energy will flow freely to try and release itself from its crystalline form, thus the process of evolution continues.'

What you need to keep in mind is that we are all Spirit manifested on earth in a physical form. If you take away the physical form we are all part of the same energy source. You need to open your mind to other forms capable of experience and intelligence that are not human to fully comprehend that we are no different from other beings around us. Unfortunately, we have a tendency to place ourselves at the top of the food chain and believe we are the most intelligent life form. We are not; we can be wiped out by something as small as a virus. We are part of the food chain and the cycle of death and renewal just like every other living being on this earth. It is a part of transformation or energy: we die and our body goes back to the earth to be transformed into something else, and our spirit travels to another realm where it remains until it chooses to experience physical reality again.

DOCTRINE OF SIGNATURES

Knowing your chakras thoroughly and what lessons they correspond to puts you well on your way to understanding what a lot of the crystals are for without having to open a book.

In my both of my herbal medicine degrees I learnt this amazing thing called the doctrine of signatures. This doctrine states that natural objects that resemble particular parts of the body can be used to treat ailments of those body parts, and that the object's location, habits, colour and form give clues as to how and when it can be used. Thus healers have come to understand the uses of herbs simply by observing the plant's conditions, locality and characteristics: its colour, where it grew, how animals used it, when it flowered etc.

Let's look at aloe vera as an example, which we know is great for sunburn. Its doctrine of signature shows that it loves the sun but is full of moisture inside. Its main action is to give moisture back to your skin after exposure to the sun.

Another strong signature is that of the ginkgo tree, the leaves of which demonstrate what it's best used for.

Ginkgo

The leaves are very similar in shape to the two lobes of the brain, the eye with its optic nerve, the kidneys and the lungs. It helps to supply blood and oxygen to all of those body parts.

In Chinese medicine, flowers that grow up and open generally work on releasing pathogens from the upper body, such as in the eyes and sinuses. Even the humble walnut, the nut of which looks like a brain, has beneficial effects on the brain. *Nature is awesome.*

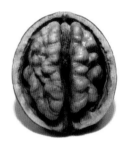

Walnut

Some indigenous tribes claim that plants have a particular song or vibration specific to each plant, that this is how they can find it, hear it and know it. This relates to the vibration theory, and I believe it is the same for crystals.

THE DOCTRINE OF SIGNATURES FOR CRYSTALS

My focus here will be mainly on quartz. I could probably write a whole book on quartz, because there are so many variations of size, shape and colour. Crystals and stones in the quartz family include rock crystal (which I address in this

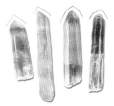

Quartz points

Single termination

Double terminated quartz

Quartz cluster

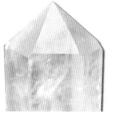

Generator crystal

chapter), citrine, amethyst, ametrine, smoky quartz, rose quartz, agate, carnelian, chalcedony, chert, tiger's eye and chrysoprase. Rock quartz also gives some great examples of the doctrine of signatures, and once you start to see them it will all start making perfect sense.

Quartz points: The point of a crystal, where all the faces of the crystal meet at the end, is called a termination. These crystals are commonly used in grids. Quartz crystals have six sides and six faces.

Single-terminated quartz: these are the most widely found and used. The energy travels from the base where it was attached to its matrix and then travels out the point.

Double-terminated quartz: the energy of these crystals travels out both ends. These crystals are good to use when you want energy to flow in both directions and for connecting two grids together or where you need an energy exchange between two objects.

Crystal clusters: this is a grouping together of the same crystals; they are all fused to a matrix at the bottom that connects them all. These formations are used for working with groups of people, particularly if you want to increase the cohesiveness and communication of a group environment. The points of each crystal within a cluster point in many different directions, so you could use it to send your intention in many directions at once or use the collective force of the many for your work.

Generator crystals: all the faces of the termination finish at one point, so the energy is very focused to come out of the tip as well as being balanced. Natural generator crystals are actually quite rare, but you will find many cut crystals claiming to be generators. Please know these do not hold the same qualities as natural generator crystals.

Laser crystal

Laser crystals: laser crystals are long, thin crystals in which the energy travels very fast with precision out of the tip.

Spheres: the energy from spheres goes out in all directions.

Quartz sphere

Elestial or skeletal quartz: there are so many types of elestial and skeletal quartz crystals it would be impossible to describe them all here, but in general these crystals exhibit specific growth features including geometric patterns, depressions and raised terminations due to their unstable conditions during crystallisation.

Elestial amethyst

An *elestial* can be recognised by the numerous small terminations that make up the larger termination or body of the crystal, helping us to understand the concept that the many make up the whole. These are good crystals to use to communicate with guides or Spirit. I look at these as though they are a group of souls connected to form the larger collectiveness. These crystals can teach us much about how to bring about positive change into the world at this time, and that many small actions can have a significant impact.

Skeletal quartz

Sceptre amethyst.

Sceptre quartz

Phantom quartz 1

Phantom quartz 2

Phantom quartz 3

Elestial crystals are also called *skeletal crystals*, although not all skeletal crystals are classed as being elestial. The skeletal layers of the crystal may not have quite finished forming, therefore you can actually see into the crystal. These crystals allow you to strip away what is not needed and see the root of an issue. They also allow you to see inside yourself without all of your layers of protection, and to see the layers of understanding needed around situations.

Sceptre crystals: sceptre crystals form when a crystal grows around another crystal. These have the power of two crystals together, but because one penetrates into the other they help you get to the heart of the matter. They also help you work on your inner self, and are one of my favourite crystals.

Phantom quartz: another of my favourites is the phantom crystal. There are lines within the crystal that are exactly the same shape at its termination, which happens when minerals or deposits grow or are captured on the outside of the crystal and the crystal continues to grow, essentially encompassing this growth. These crystals allow you to look at patterns regarding your growth and stages of evolution, and at lessons that may still need to be learned inside you. They also encompass the mineral that grows on them and is now inside, taking on the qualities of that mineral or crystal.

Self-healed crystals: is it any wonder this is a favourite? These crystals have been broken or snapped off their matrix and then healed where they were broken. Where the break would have been you will see small terminations of regrowth. I think the doctrine of signatures speaks for itself with this one. These are such beautiful and powerful crystals to work with because ultimately we all need to heal ourselves.

Self-healed crystal

Natural vs cut vs polished: my preference is for natural and polished crystals, although I do have cut crystals and make wands and jewellery with them. You will feel what is right for you and what is not, but what is the difference? On a single-terminated quartz crystal the energy travels from the base up to the tip due to the molecular structure within the crystal, which flows in a particular direction. When a crystal is cut into the same shape the internal structure is not the same and the energy doesn't flow in the same direction as that of a natural crystal. There are always exceptions, however.

Natural vs Cut

Crystal researcher Marcel Vogel, a senior scientist with IBM for 27 years, discovered that when quartz is cut into a particular shape with very specific angles, which he termed a Vogel, it took on particular qualities. These crystals are cut along the axis that will allow the energy to flow normally through the crystal. True Vogels are still cut today by the men who worked with Vogel in their now respective businesses, but you can find cheaper versions in many places. If you are purchasing inexpensive Vogels there may be big differences.

Vogel

This is not an authentic Vogel, although it has been cut from a single-terminated quartz crystal, as it has a phantom inside. This shows the direction of the flow within the crystal, but it has been cut slightly off-centre. I use this one for healings and as a single-terminated crystal, not a double-terminated or Vogel crystal.

I have also come across supposed sceptre and twin crystals that have been cut to that shape from one chunk of quartz. When you get to know your crystals these types of things become very noticeable, but there are many good fakes on the market. Crystals are lab created, heat treated, dyed and even glued onto a matrix to look attractive to the unsuspecting buyer; they may gain other qualities or just be void of any form of positive energy. The more you can tune into your instincts instead of a compulsive buying habit the better you will be at picking what's right and what's not.

Rough vs polished crystals: 'rough' refers to a crystal as you would find it in nature. Many quartz points are polished up to make them look more appealing, especially if they have been damaged in any way to start with. This is still okay, as polishing out a chip here and there doesn't alter the qualities of the crystals. Crystals can be polished up to expose even more of their natural beauty, but sometimes this polishing process is taken too far with the need to mass market and create as much profit as possible.

No thought, feeling or love is put into their creation, and this is not what the industry should be about. You can feel when a stone or crystal has been mistreated, and it is possible to care for it and give energy back to it. Give it love or your attention just as you would to a plant, animal or human. Sometimes you cannot change what has been done, but you can make a difference when it has come to your attention.

HOW CRYSTALS ARE USED

I use quartz in all my grids, and you can create grids with quartz alone. It is the easiest crystal to find and can be used to substitute any other crystal you need. I'll explain that in more detail later on. Quartz is also known as the 'master crystal'.

Quartz is silicon dioxide that has long been used in radios, watches and computers. Quartz is termed 'piezoelectric', which means that when pressure is applied it will emit an electrical charge. Also, if an electrical charge is sent to it it will bend or slightly change its shape. Due to its incredibly stable structure, quartz possesses a high and exact rate of vibration, properties that make it invaluable as a timekeeper and the reason it was used in watches to keep accurate time. Quartz is abundant in geographical fault lines, so can you imagine the charge it puts out when compressed under such stress from the earth shifting?

Quartz emits negative ions, which are very beneficial for your health. Just as with ionisers or salt lamps they attract positive ions, which essentially are broken ions. Negative ions can draw out positive ions and remove them from your energy field.

Quartz has a high vibration and the tendency to raise the vibrations of whatever it comes into contact with, so having it close to you or holding it can have a positive effect on you.

Quartz amplifies energy, so if you are using any form of energy healing it will increase this work.

Marcel Vogel said in Richard Gerber's book *Vibrational Medicine* (Inner Traditions – Bear and Company, 2001): '... the crystal emits a vibration which extends and amplifies the powers of the user's mind. Like a laser, it radiates energy in a coherent, highly concentrated form and this energy may be transmitted into objects or people at will.' Gerber goes on to say that Vogel explains how 'the quartz crystal is capable of amplifying and directing the natural energies of the healer'.

Also from Gerber's book, quoting Vogel:

> 'The psychic healer has to deal with the emanations of his hand or of his bioenergy field, which do not have the same levels of coherency one can obtain by using a crystal. The crystal works much the same way that a laser does: it takes scattered rays of energy and makes the energy field so coherent and unidirectional that a tremendous force is generated ...'

One morning I woke up and received an image in my head of an elemental being holding out a double-terminated quartz crystal to me. She called it 'the gift'. This truly was a gift, and I received the reason why at the same time: it was to convey the knowledge to me that crystals are communication tools that open up clear communication like a two-way radio. They bridge the gap to the other worlds. This image left such an impact on me I had to draw the elemental being and I knew I had to share this knowledge at some point.

Their communicative quality means quartz can be used to substitute any crystal you do not have. Just as crystal spirits and guides can work through specific stones, so too can you call on a specific crystal spirit to work through your quartz stone. You might want to work with black tourmaline but don't have any, however, you do have a quartz crystal or tumble stone so you can ask the black tourmaline crystal spirit to please communicate to you through the quartz crystal. It can be a small tumble stone, which are readily available and easy to carry with you; you don't have to have an extensive crystal library. Quartz is really all you need to get started.

MEGALITHIC SITES AND QUARTZ

It is possible that the people who created megalithic structures understood certain qualities of quartz and similar stones. They could also have placed these stones protruding into the earth because they wanted to communicate with the ancestors or spirits of those who had passed. Megalithic structures served many purposes and here we uncover some very interesting facts.

Archeologists have discovered that most known megalithic structures around Europe are made up of quartz-bearing rocks. These rocks were either cut and transported over long distances or cut into rock on site. An interesting article by academician Ruslan L. Kostov explains that the distribution of these sites corresponds to where quartz-bearing rocks are located.[*]

Figure 1. Distribution of megalithic sites on the British Isles (Chippindale, 1983); examples of clustering at the Cornwall Peninsula, Isle of Arran, eastern Scotland and Northern Ireland, areas of granite and other quartz-bearing rocks.

Figure 2. Distribution of megalithic monuments (left) in France and location of acid intrusive (granite) or metamorphic (mainly gneiss) rocks (right).

Figure 3. Distribution of megalithic monuments (left) in Portugal and localisation of acid igneous intrusive (granite, granodiorite, tonalite) and volcanic rocks (right).

The same seems to be true for Spain, Bulgaria, South-East Asia and the Pacific region.

Koslov also states:

◊ In the Carnac area in Brittany, France, the orientations of the dolmens (a megalithic monument consisting of a horizontal stone slab on top of two or more upright stones) coincide with the orientation of the fault lines, which may suggest they are linked to the qualities of seismic, electric, magnetic and gravitational activity. This is also true for the dolmens in the Western Caucasus, in Southern Russia, which are linked to large faults.

◊ White quartz pebbles may have been used in moon rituals.

◊ There also seems to be certain acoustic properties within megalithic sites due to the arrangement of the stones. Whether this was intended or not remains a mystery.

---

* Ruslan I. Kostov, 'Geological and Mineralogical background of the Megalithic and rock-cut sites in Bulgaria and some other European Countries', in R.I. Kostov, B. Gaydarska, M. Gurova (eds), 2008 *International Conference on Geoarchaeology and Archaeomineralogy.* "St Ivan Rilski", Sofia, pp163–168.

Many quartz crystals and quartz crystal skulls have been found at megalithic sites around the world.

It has long been believed that ancient civilisations had advanced knowledge of the principles of nature. It is still not known how many megalithic sites around the world were constructed, let alone how blocks of precision-cut stones weighing tonnes were moved over great distances and placed within millimetres of accuracy to align with very specific angles and degrees.

One theory that resonates is the theory that ancient civilisations used specific sounds or vibrations, known as acoustic levitation. The fact that they used quartz-bearing stones with very specific qualities lends credence to the idea that sound and quartz played an integral role in their construction.

An incredibly skilled inventor in the 1800s, John Keely, claimed he could crumble quartz just through the use of sound. He also worked on many anti-gravity theories. It is said that Tibetan monks could move large stone blocks through the use of certain musical instruments, rendering the blocks almost weightless through the vibration of the instruments. This may be a forgotten natural law that science is yet to rediscover, or it may be lost along with those civilisations.

My point is that quartz is extremely important to us and to nature; it is not just simply a rock. It is because of its amazing properties we use it so much in our grids and for healing work.

CHAKRA CRYSTALS

If you look at the doctrine of signatures you can see that the colour of a stone or crystal corresponds with the colour of each chakra, which is an easy way to remember what each stone or crystal is used for. Crystals can have many uses, so this is just a basic guide. I have listed the stones that may be useful for each chakra in the colours I mentioned earlier, from red to white; however, you may feel that violet and purple stones are for the crown and indigo stones are for the third eye.

Don't be limited by my explanations; just use what feels right for you as it is the intent that is what is most important here. I have included the stones I personally own here, but there are many more you might like to use. Don't feel you have to acquire everything, as some of these crystals may be difficult to find. You might want to get a stone of every colour to work with, and tumble stones are great for this. Not only are they readily available, but they are also affordable.

I have a collection of different varieties of quartz to make up the chakra colours. From left to right they are red quartz, yellow quartz, green prasem quartz, blue indicolite-included quartz, amethyst and clear quartz.

I have found pastel or light colours to be very gentle, that they seem to work very subtly on the energy fields with love. They are like a higher vibration within their colour range. Darker-coloured crystals can give a more intense experience. For example, when you see a pastel baby pink colour you may feel a very gentle love, while a deep raspberry pink colour will have a more intense feel to it. Keep this in mind when choosing stones for your grids or healing: sometimes you need very gentle energy to help you and sometimes you need something a bit stronger.

Red crystals: base chakra

From far left: red jasper, garnet, red tiger's eye, mookaite, dragon stone, ruby, red agate (centre).

Orange crystals: sacral chakra

From far left: heat-treated citrine, stilbite, orange kyanite, sputnik aragonite, copper, tangerine quartz, peach moonstone, sunstone, carnelian, orange calcite (centre).

Yellow crystals: solar plexus chakra

From far left: yellow quartz, Libyan tektite, sulphur-included quartz, chalcopyrite, pyrite, hiddenite, honey calcite, heat-treated citrine tumble stone, orange calcite (centre).

Green crystals: heart chakra

From middle far left, middle: seraphinite, amazonite, fuschite, prehnite, green calcite, chrysoprase, grossularite, malachite, prehnite, jade (large chunk), serpentine (under the jade), epidote, green kyanite and green tourmaline.

Pink crystals: heart chakra

From far left: pink agate limb cast, clinozoisite, pink chalcedony, rhodochrosite, mangano calcite, pink petrified wood, rose quartz, pink kunzite, pink tourmaline (below the pink kunzite), cobalto calcite (centre).

Blue crystals: throat chakra

From far left: azurite, lapis lazuli, shattuckite, blue kyanite, apatite, K2, angelite, hemimorphite, aragonite, blue fluorite, dumortierite, iolite, blue tiger's eye, covellite, aquamarine (centre left), aqua aura quartz (centre right; man-altered), indolite (blue tourmaline) in quartz (centre bottom).

Purple crystals: third eye chakra

From far left: amethyst, pink kunzite, purple fluorite, lepidolite, charoite, chevron amethyst, amethyst tumble stone, amethyst sceptre (centre).

White or clear crystals: crown chakra

From far left: ulexite, scolecite, clear quartz tumble stone, white calcite, quartz, stalactite quartz, sceptre quartz, selenite, menalite (centre).

Other colours

You might wonder about brown, black, and multicoloured crystals, and whether or not they have a use.

Brown crystals: these are very earthen in colour and help you to ground to the earth. They are wonderful when all your energy is in your head or you are feeling a bit spaced out, so you need to ground your energy. Working on a computer or doing a lot of mental work uses a lot of energy

in the head, so when you ground yourself you bring this energy back down and into a balanced state. Brown crystals are great to use when meditating or journeying to keep you grounded.

From far left: chiastolite, shaman stone, smoky quartz, dravite, amulet stone, petrified wood, ammonite, coffee moonstone, septarian nodule (centre).

Black crystals: black is the result of the complete absorption of visible light. Black stones absorb all of the colours of the spectrum and they also absorb energy. They are very protective and grounding stones and are great to absorb negative energy.

From far left: black tourmaline, black tourmaline tumble stone, tumbled apache tear, hematite, onyx tumble stone, black calcite.

Multicoloured crystals: look at what colours are contained in multicoloured crystals and match them up with their respective chakra. They may aid in linking chakras together, so you can work on both of them at once. This category includes quartz with inclusions. These crystals are great for amplifying the crystal or stone that has grown into the quartz crystal.

From far left: quartz with epidote, double-terminated quartz with hematite inclusions (pink and dark grey), quartz with lepidolite (top right), indicolite quartz (blue tourmaline inclusions), celadonite phantom quartz.

Quartz Inclusions

OTHER GRID ELEMENTS

There are many energies from nature besides crystals you can call to your grid, such as bird feathers, animal bones, leaves, twigs, flowers and shells. Each of these elements hold their own vibration and call their archetypal energy to the grid. For example, you can use a feather to bring the qualities of the bird it belongs to, or a branch for the specific tree energy it has. You can create an entire grid from nature elements! Do not underestimate the power of working with other elements in this manner: everything is from the one Source. You must always work respectfully with nature, so please use only what you need and ask the plant or being if you may pick a part of it for your grid. Look for fallen objects, and when finished with your grid either leave it to the elements or pack it up and place it back in nature, giving the beings your gratitude for working with you. You might feel more inclined to work with these energies due to environmental reasons, and I urge you to explore this area.

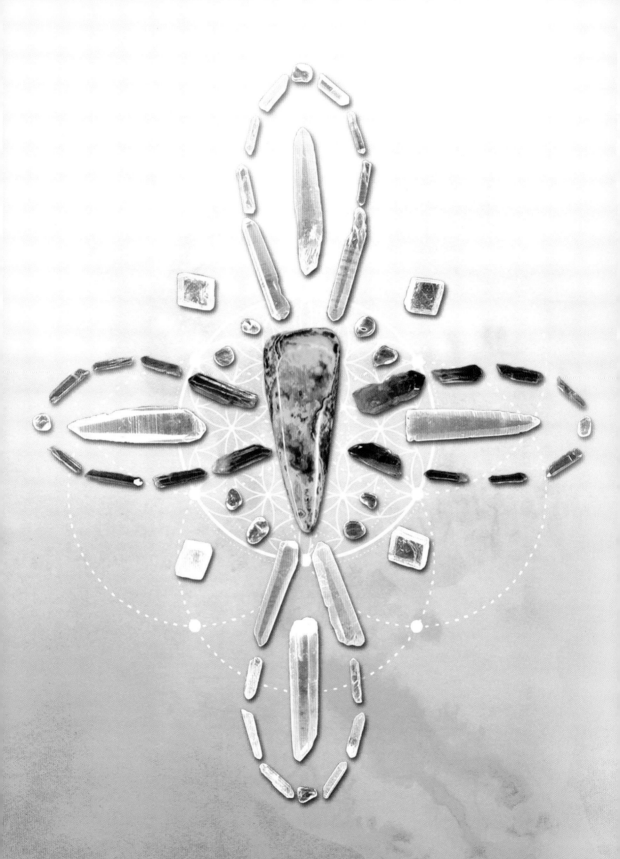

CHAPTER 6

SACRED GEOMETRY AND GRID TEMPLATES

As already discussed, geometric shapes are the building blocks of nature; *everything* is formed by vibration and geometry. Geometry is the way in which universal energy manifests in the physical plane and essentially how it communicates to every living thing on earth. This, in turn, may be the way in which we can communicate back.

You can work with specific geometric shapes because they each have their own vibratory pattern. Remember that the geometric shape of a Chladni image is actually a cross section of a larger 3D object. When you place your crystals on a crystal grid cloth, board or image, because the crystals are in such close proximity to each other they have overlapping and interconnected energy fields, which creates a very dynamic energy force.

There are many different geometric shapes but we will focus on a few of the main universal geometric ones and again apply the doctrine of signatures.

LEY LINES AND THE EARTH GRID

The ley line theory has been around since the 1920s. Ley lines are a series of unseen lines that reportedly connect megalithic structures. Some people believe ley lines hold the energies of the earth, although scientists doubt their existence. Some theories suggest megalithic structures were built as signposts or markers across the landscape and that they aligned in a straight line. Other theories say the monuments are aligned to ley lines, which hold specific energies due to quartz-bearing rocks and are powered by geographical fault lines and volcanic activity. The standing stones then became areas in which energy was channelled. It does seem that our ancestors had a great understanding of the earth's energies and how to harness them.

Is there a grid around the earth? This is a subject that is largely debated; however, mention of the grid has been handed down through many different cultures including the Australian Aborigines and Native Americans. They say it is vitally important for this grid to be maintained and strengthened. You can research the many earth grid theories and maps for yourself and make up your own mind what resonates with you. The grid might not be something that can be mapped if it is energetic. Many people researching ley lines use dowsing rods and claim to be able to locate and follow them.

If there is a grid around or in the earth, why is it important? Is it possible for us to tap into or harness the energies of this grid for ourselves like our ancestors may have done? If we know where ley lines are, can we create healing grids there that can be amplified?

You may be located far away from any standing stone, circle or ley line, but I will take you through a meditation later that will allow you to tap into this source and supercharge your grid.

CRYSTAL GRID TEMPLATES

I hope by now you can see a theme developing of how you can choose the right tools for your grid to align with your intention. We'll dive deeper into intention setting soon, but essentially it's all about the law of attraction and gathering together many items of like energy for your goal.

Here we look closer into what type of geometric design you might choose for your grid. There are many crystal grid templates you can purchase to place your crystals on, from cloth to wooden ones. You can also just as easily print one off or draw one yourself. The main aim is to have a template so you know where to place your crystals, although it is not a necessity: it merely adds another layer and makes your grids look really pretty. Here are a few you might like to use.

The flower of life: the flower of life image can be seen all around the world in temples, manuscripts and art. You will even find it in Leonardo da Vinci's journals. When you think of a flower you think of a seed or a beginning that with the right elements for growth will flower into life and blossom. The centre circle in the image replicates itself over and over, which could be a repeated pattern with no end.

I use this grid when I want a project to blossom or I am looking for growth and success; I remember it as bringing something to life. I also see it as representing the idea that many make up the whole and everything is connected.

Metatron's cube: all geometric patterns can be derived from the flower of life, and Metatron's cube is where we start.

Metatron's cube contains within it the five platonic solids.

The platonic solids are 3D objects that have the same shape on all sides. For example, a cube is made up of six equal squares, a tetrahedron is made from three equal triangles, a dodecahedron is made from 12 equal pentagons and so on.

The platonic solids are said to be the building blocks of life and are commonly found in nature, in minerals, sound and organic life forms, for example.

I use this grid when I need answers to something I am working on or to acquire what I need to create something. I also use it when I need to gather information or to find the building blocks needed for a particular issue or project. It can be used for growth and stability, as it contains everything necessary to create structure. It is also said to be a symbol that wards off negative energy, so it is useful for protection grids or for deflecting energy.

Fibonacci spiral: this grid uses the mathematical Fibonacci sequence, a series of numbers that create spirals and squares in an ever-increasing and repeating pattern. I use this grid to increase energy. If you have an intention or project that you want to snowball or just get increasingly bigger, this is your grid. There are many uses for this grid; you may want to: increase your network of friends or associates within your field; increase your feelings of love or gratitude; or have your finished project really take off and get itself out there.

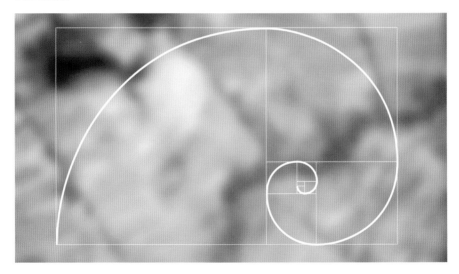

The medicine wheel: this is a very popular grid formation that is used around the world by many cultures, such as the Native Americans and Celts. Essentially it represents the four directions of north, east, south and west. Each direction on the medicine wheel also has its own element: earth, fire, water and air. The hemisphere you live in will determine where the elements are placed, that is, in the northern hemisphere south represents fire, whereas in the southern hemisphere north represents fire. It is hottest at the equator, so wherever you are, locate the fire element facing it.

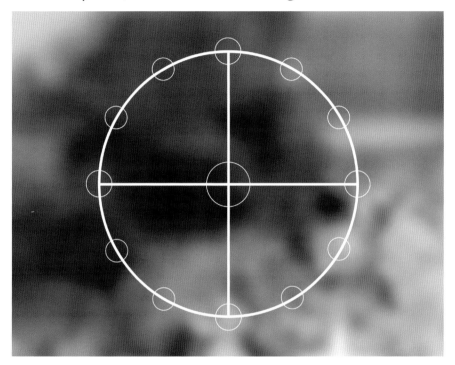

The medicine wheel can also represent the four seasons and specific animals or deities.

A set of lessons comes with each direction, and you can also seek help or insight into any issues you are facing. These grids when created outside are generally made from large stones rather than crystals. If you have a large one outside, walk around the circle until you feel the right direction to sit in. If you already know which direction you need, sit in that part of the circle and ask for guidance or meditate or journey there. You can create a grid from crystals to sit and meditate in; whether inside or outside these are very powerful.

You don't have to orientate your grid to the true direction if it is going to be inside or on an altar. It's about intent so any layout you use is fine. You can place something at each point to represent each element or direction.

Use this grid to ask for help from the elements or directions or any of the animals or deities of your beliefs that you honour with it. You can use it to send a message to all four corners of the earth as it is a very powerful grid. You must always honour and respect the elemental beings if you choose to ask them for help. You must always come from a place of love and respect to work with these energies or they will refuse to work with you; they cannot be fooled.

Infinity symbol: just as the name suggests, this grid is great to use for something you want to continuously manifest with no end date. Many use this for abundance so they can keep on manifesting it repeatedly. Green stones and citrine are traditionally used to manifest abundance, so can be of great use in abundance grids. Green is significant in feng shui for abundance and citrine is beneficial because it works on your sacral chakra, which is your relationship to money chakra.

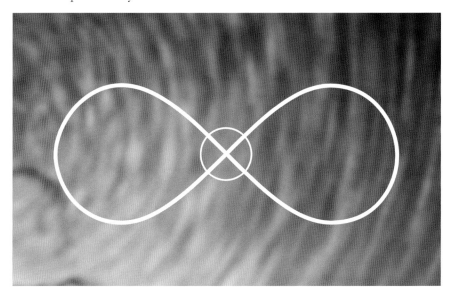

Intuitive grid: is it necessary to stick to a grid structure? No, it's not, and you don't always have to work with sacred geometry. Even just a simple circle is a geometric shape, and clearly an important one in nature and with the medicine wheel, the flower of life and for spellcasting. If you feel intuitively guided to create a shape or arrange your crystals in a certain way then do it. Always trust in your intuition. Always remember that it is all about intent, and when you combine certain items together for a specific purpose they resonate together. It is also another good way of getting to know your crystals and working with how they wish to be used. As you can see by my light bringer card there is no particular geometric grid; however, I have made it symmetrical.

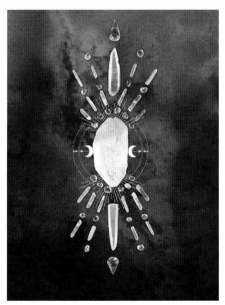 

My crystal grid oracle was created completely by intuition. Every grid I arranged I did through intuition, and when I wrote the guidebook I was amazed at how everything made sense! For example:

Protection: notice how the black tourmaline crystals are on the outside, creating a perimeter. Tourmaline is a very protective stone that shows you how to put up a barrier to protect yourself.

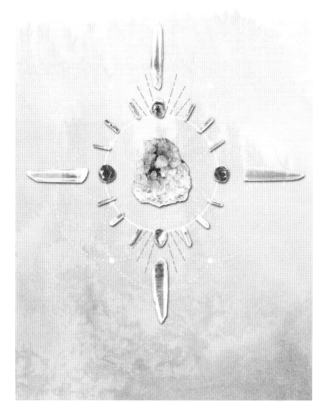

Self-love: a simple grid with cobalto calcite in the centre. The focus is on the centre stone because the grid's main focus is you and loving yourself first.

Other inspiration: you might also be inspired to create a grid pattern from other sources, such as the patterns you find in nature or symbols that mean something to you. Use your imagination and intuition to create something unique.

Pentagram: the pentagram is a pagan symbol representing the interconnectedness of the five elements: fire, earth, air, water and spirit/ether. Interestingly, in Chinese medicine the five element theory also uses the pentagram to represent their five elements and their interconnectedness: fire, earth, metal, water and wood.

Pentagrams represent how each element is reliant on the other and how it is a never-ending, repeated cycle. I use this grid for many things: to bring balance into my life or stability from the ups and downs, and to work with the elements of nature when I want to create a grid to connect to nature. It has also been a symbol commonly used for protection and to ward off negative energy. It is a great symbol to use in gridding if you need protection of any sort, or it can be placed in an area to deflect unwanted energies.

It is certainly not a symbol to ever be afraid of. It has only gained a stigma through misinterpretation and the use of it in horror films. It does have an air of mysticism around it that draws people to it. Every symbol has its own signature vibration; you are drawn to particular symbols for a reason, and this may be because it resonates with you on an energetic level.

Septagram (heptagram): the septagram is largely known these days as the elven or fairy star; however, it is only a very recent adoption of the symbol. The symbol first showed itself in the Kabbalah and also in Christianity to represent the seven days of creation and protection. Alchemists believe it represents the seven planets, while others believe it represents the seven directions of north, east, south, west, above, below and within. Whatever your reason for using the septagram or heptagram, believe in your intent. If you wish to use it to connect to the fae, do so; if you use it for its astrological symbolism, do so. Make it what you want it to be, as it is your intent that is the main focus.

Room grid: you can create a grid around your room by placing crystals in each corner. You might have a healing room where you would like to create a harmonious environment or a study area in which you wish to receive spiritual guidance. I have gridded my bedroom with black tourmaline and black moonstone to help with my sleep. It is important to note that quartz can keep you awake at night due to its high vibration and specific qualities already mentioned. For this reason I tend not to use it in the bedroom unless it is next to a big chunk of tourmaline to increase the energy of the tourmaline. I placed the moonstone as the centre crystal under my bed and the tourmaline and quartz in each corner of the room.

House grid: you can even grid your home! When I have wanted to stay grounded and have a calming home away from external influences I have gridded my home with black tourmaline and quartz. You never know where you're going to come across my crystals at home; you might find them in the pantry or in cupboards!

Property grid: there could be many reasons for gridding an entire property. You might want to create a particular energy, one that is full of peace, protection or abundance. Whatever the reason, you will need larger stones or many small stones. Place the crystals in each corner of the boundary and the main one in the middle of the property. If the property is very large, you might want to place smaller crystals along the boundary line, staggered every metre or so.

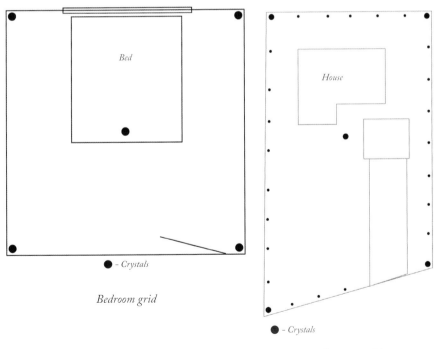

● - *Crystals*

Bedroom grid

● - *Crystals*

Property grid

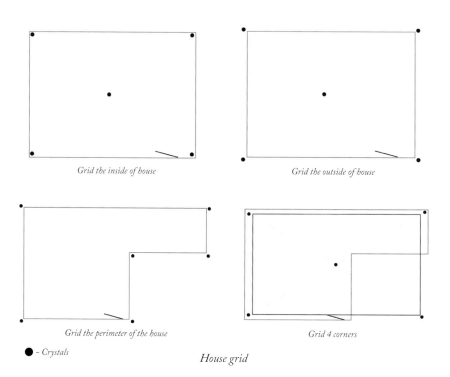

Grid the inside of house

Grid the outside of house

Grid the perimeter of the house

Grid 4 corners

● - Crystals

House grid

SAMPLE GRID LAYOUTS

Chakra layout grid: what about a total chakra balance layout? Or you could do a simple one chakra crystal grid if you want to work on a particular chakra.

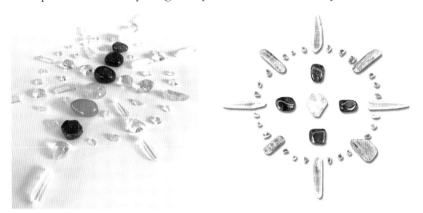

Love grid: here you can see I have chosen pink for my love grid because it is a heart chakra stone. I have also used the flower of life grid under my crystals because I want it to grow and multiply. I've used the very gentle baby pink crystals as I want it to be a gentle, loving grid.

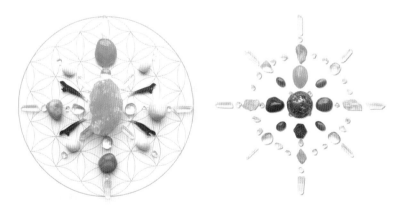

Abundance grid: I have chosen red, orange and yellow stones for my abundance grid, as I want to work on my base chakra for survival (money), my sacral chakra (relationship to money) and my solar plexus chakra (my self-esteem and if I feel deserving of money).

Shamanic or Celtic grids: This is the grid I use to contact the ancestors. You may like a grid that represents your heritage and helps you to connect to yours. Keep in mind the ancestors are not just your blood lineage; it is a term used to contact those who have gone before you. For this grid I used:

Preseli bluestone is the stone that the inner circle of Stonehenge is made from, and it comes from only one place: Preseli Hills in west Wales. Stonehenge is also thought to have been used to contact ancestors, hence why I used Preseli bluestone for the centre crystal. Celtic Ogham staves are small sticks from each of the different trees that correspond to each Ogham symbol. This is an ancient tree language and calls the energies of each tree to the grid. I find this a powerful grid for asking for guidance and connecting with the ancestors.

Triskele or triskelion: this ancient Irish Celtic symbol that appeared on the Newgrange kerbstones as far back as 3200 BC. There is speculation around its true interpretation, although it is said to represent earth, water and sky/spiritual, physical and celestial/past, present, future/life, death and rebirth. The symbol has a movement aspect to it, like a rolling wave. To me it represents the cycles of all things and the continual flow, movement and evolution. This would be an amazing grid to use to set things in motion, to help you go with the flow and to connect to your own cycles.

Triquetra or Trinity knot: this Celtic symbol has been adopted by many cultures, each of which has their own set of beliefs so it has no definite meaning. Like the triskele, the triquetra has three parts to it and is seen to represent the same elements along with representing continuity and the flow of life. It is found both with and without a circle in it. Circles and Celtic knotwork represent infinity, due to there being no start and no end.

Distance healing grid: the beautiful thing about energy work is that it is not limited to time and space. Even if you live far away from anyone, you can still do this work wherever you are and have a positive effect on someone's life. First, you must ask the person's permission to do so; it is important that you never direct energy to anyone without their permission. You can use a photograph of them in the grid to help visualise and direct the energy to them, or something that is personal to them to bring their energy to the grid and help connect it to them.

CRYSTAL GRID ELIXIRS OR ESSENCES

This is a beautiful area you might want to explore for yourself. Just like flower essences, you can make up crystal essences from your grids. If you place water in a glass container within your crystal grid it will become infused with the energy from the grid. This essence can then be taken internally to reap more benefits from your grid.

You can also send the essence to the person you created a distance healing grid for, or you can make up mother tinctures of each different chakra colour to work on your chakras one at a time. The uses are only limited by your imagination. If this really interests you, head to my website (www.spiritstone. com.au) for my mini gem elixir ebook to get you started.

PLACEMENT OF CRYSTALS ON YOUR GRID

There is no right or wrong way to place your crystals, but there are a few things you should do to make it all gel. Start your crystal grids with a centre crystal, which will be chosen for its qualities of being able to work with your intent. (Manifestation and intention setting are covered in Chapter 7.) You may have picked the centre crystal based on its corresponding chakra, or you may have another reason. The centre crystal is usually the largest, and what you are aiming to do is to link all the surrounding crystals to it.

The energy of quartz travels in the direction of its termination, so you should use quartz crystals to determine the direction of the energy in the grid. If you use tumble stones the direction is multidirectional, so these will generally amplify the energy of the grid in an unspecific direction.

If I use a grid template I normally begin by placing my main crystal in the centre and then place four or so medium-sized stones on the outside. You can use quartz points at each corner of the circle or other stones you have chosen to complement your main stone.

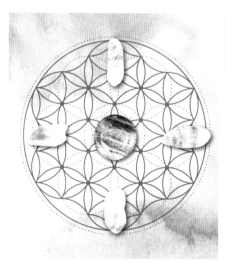
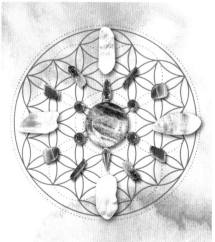

To start your layout, place the smaller crystals on the intersections of the grid then add the extra crystals around them.

If I don't use a template I always still start with the centre crystal and then place the other four crystals. These four crystals help me with creating symmetry in my grid and act like a guide so I can figure out where to place the rest.

You also need to take into account the direction of the crystals. To use a simple love grid as an example: if you want to create a beautiful loving atmosphere in a room, you might put rose quartz in the centre of the grid and then place the quartz points facing away from the centre to direct the energy of the quartz into the room and surrounds.

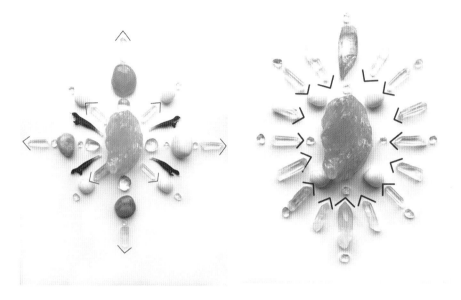

If you want to find love, you might face the crystals in towards the centre to increase its intensity and ask the spirit of rose quartz to help you find love.

You might be wondering what the difference is, but this book is not intended to give you all the answers. It is a guide only, and you must always use your intuition over anything else. It will all come together in the chapter on activating your grid. Activating your grid is *the* most important step, because this is the part where you connect to it and ask all the energies to help you with your intention. Otherwise your grid simply becomes a pretty rock formation and nothing else.

Medicine wheel grid: In my crossroads card, I used the classic medicine wheel layout and placed the quartz points facing outwards. If you are seeking guidance from the directions you may want to create a medicine wheel grid to sit in and have the points facing yourself in the centre. You might want to have tumble stones at each direction or, if the grid is outside, you could plant your quartz points into the ground with the point facing up. Sit in the centre and feel if you are drawn to a particular direction, then place a large crystal at that direction only. Always follow what you feel guided to do, even if you are unsure. The more you practise, the stronger this sense will become.

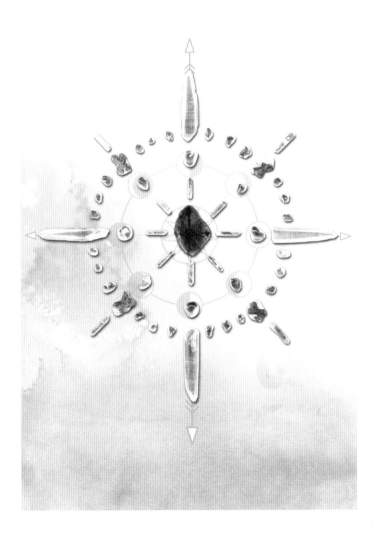

Infinity grid: the quartz points in the infinity grid can be directed along its lines. Place the centre crystal right in the middle, or place one in each open space. I used this grid for my deep healing card.

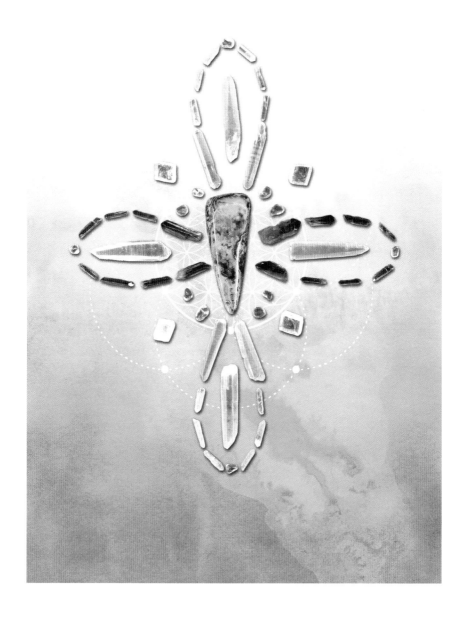

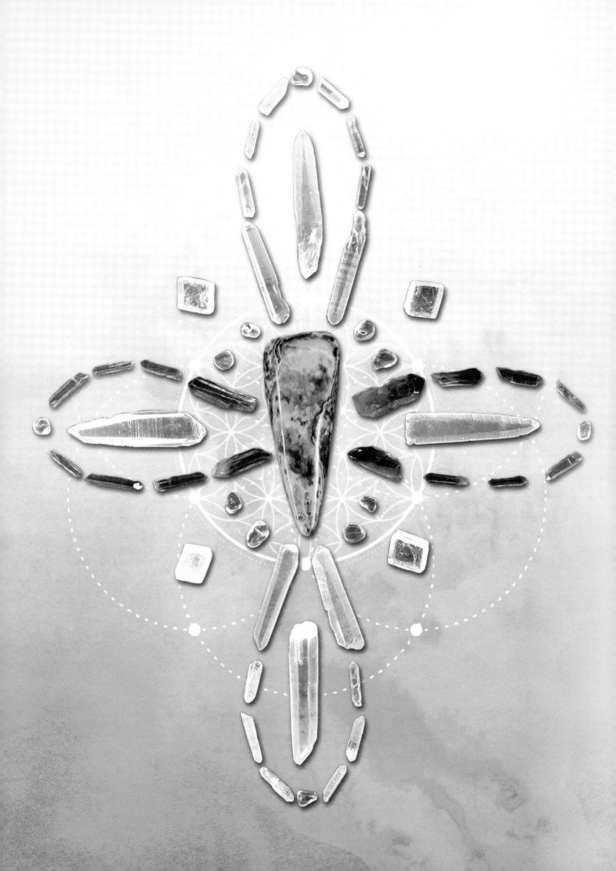

CHAPTER 7

MANIFESTATION AND INTENTION SETTING

*'The universe makes way for those
who know where they are going.'*

We have covered chakras, choosing crystals, deciding on layouts and placement of crystals, but it can't all come together if you don't have a clear focus or intention on what you want to manifest. One great thing about coming from the corporate world is that I learnt many planning techniques that can be applied to any issue in life. I've adjusted them slightly and made them my own. I find this technique of creating an intention pivotal in manifesting real change. Here's where you get down into the nitty-gritty.

KEYS TO MANIFESTATION

These are my three keys to manifestation:

◊ The thought process: define your goal or intention; the where do you want to be?

◊ The spiritual process: set forth your intention through ritual, whether that be meditation, crystal grids or any other way in which you call on Spirit; connect with Source energy.

◊ The physical process: take action on the information you receive; the how do you get there?

Only by truly looking at yourself with no judgement can you really create a change within yourself and your environment. We tend to assume we know what we want in life, but who actually writes a list of what they want to achieve? It's surprising to note that even if you write a list of the things you would like to achieve through the year, unless you actively work to achieve those things not many of them will get ticked off by the end of the year.

Sometimes just setting the intention and focusing on what you want will be enough. We live in a physical world, so there are things we need to physically do ourselves. You cannot solely rely on the universe to drop everything into your lap. If it were that easy, you wouldn't be here now learning this reality. The universe also can't bring you what you want unless you know what it is. I love the saying: 'The universe makes way for those who know where they are going.' When you start to define where you want to go, the law of attraction will start bringing you more of what you need to get you there.

Along the way you will sometimes hit roadblocks to achieving your dreams, but you need to start looking at these more as lessons you need to work through before you can move to the next level. You are here to grow and learn lessons; if there were no lessons, how would you evolve? Sometimes you'll feel it is just blow after blow and get exhausted from the life lessons, but the lessons have shaped you and you will be able to navigate them better as you age.

We are living in an age of extreme growth. Because of the vast amount of knowledge available in the form of the internet, social media, books, courses and teachers we are experiencing accelerated growth in our mental, spiritual and emotional bodies. This is a big reason for why our physical bodies are not coping as well, together with other things such as increased workloads, being time poor, inadequate diets and world events and stressors like we have never known.

You need to be clear on what you want to manifest. What do you truly want in your life, and are you prepared to look at what's needed to achieve those goals? You have to be real. If you really want something in your life but are not prepared to let go of whatever is blocking you from achieving it, then your manifestation will fall short.

Life is all about growth and learning. Manifestation can introduce lessons you need to work on in order to achieve this growth and essentially manifest your desires. Once you have learnt a lesson in this lifetime you don't need to repeat it in your next; I always remind myself of this and ask, do I want to keep repeating this pattern forever? Do I want to come back next lifetime and go through it all again? No! Then it's up to me to do the work. Will you learn all the lessons you are here for in this lifetime? Maybe; maybe not.

I have had an ongoing health issue that has plagued me my whole life, and I feel at times that I'm never going to be well. I have fibromyalgia, the symptoms of which include chronic fatigue and pain. Maybe the lesson I need to learn is to live with it instead of fighting it, or maybe the lesson was to take up a healing career. Perhaps I am capable of getting better if I stop focusing on not being able to do things like everyone else, or maybe I am still missing something and it will all become clear on my deathbed. I don't want to have to have it again in the next lifetime, as this lifetime has been incredibly hard and all I want is a body that works like a normal one. I always imagine what I could achieve if I was like everyone else.

My point is that sometimes our lessons elude us our whole life and may never resolve or need to be resolved. This may lead you to think your manifestation hasn't worked, when in fact it might have led you to the next step in that lesson or helped you find someone or something that took you in another direction. That's still okay. From my experience not all lessons are easy to overcome, so don't get disheartened. You may learn many lessons just from having one issue in your life that you don't understand, and perhaps that is the lesson!

Another reason why your manifestation might have failed is because it is not aligned with your higher purpose. How do you know what your higher purpose is and if you are trying to go against it? This is a whole book in itself and I am definitely no authority. One thing I have noticed is that when you help or guide others to achieve what they want, you receive what you are wanting and also the guidance you need. What you put out is what you get back; you manifest what you are. Keep this in mind if you are doing any sort of business planning. Always ask yourself: 'How does this *help* my customer?'

It is important to set yourself goals that you feel you can achieve. I cannot stress the importance of really defining your goal. It doesn't matter how big or small your goal is; you have to define it and *believe* it. If you set your goal to acquire one million dollars and deep down your core belief is saying you can't achieve that, that you're not good enough, then you won't be able to manifest it.

'Our beliefs and our intentions must be in alignment.'

There could be many other reasons why you can't manifest what you want. Perhaps manifesting one million dollars wouldn't help you with your life purpose. You might need to learn how to make money to shift your beliefs about money. Maybe if you had that money you would not focus on what you are currently doing, or maybe by manifesting that one million dollars you would be forced out of the comfort zone in which you have used the excuse that money was the only issue. When you eventually decide on your intention statement you'll need to sit with it and see how you truly feel about it. You'll notice if it makes you uncomfortable or if you wholeheartedly feel you can do it. You need to take notice of even the slightest doubt, because that will lead you to what is holding you back.

GETTING STARTED

If you are unfamiliar with it, a good way to begin manifesting is to start with something basic and achievable, such as a beautiful peaceful environment within yourself or in your home. Let's look at where to start.

Manifesting is such a personal and powerful practice. When you look deeply into exactly what you want to manifest you are saying to your soul you want something to change. All the answers lie within you, and when you start looking more and more within yourself you'll become more in control of your life. You can then take ownership of your health, career and relationships and ultimately you'll feel more grounded and content and happier with your direction in life.

Defining exactly what you want and looking at it closely before you set your intention ensures you start aligning your thoughts and beliefs. Here are some examples of what you might want to manifest:

◊   I wish to find love.
◊   I would like to find an answer to ... (You might be searching for answers or direction.)
◊   I want to bring a more harmonious flow into my life.
◊   I feel I need protection from negative influences.
◊   I would like more abundance in my life.

◊   I need help with finding the right career.

◊   I need the courage to leave my current situation.

◊   I would like to get my creativity flowing.

◊   I would like to work on increasing my spirituality.

◊   I would like healing for a specific health issue.

◊   I would like success in my business.

When setting your intentions, you need to look closely at what you are asking for. Remember that the universe will bring you exactly what you have asked for, but it might not be in the form you wanted. Why? Let's take a look at the above examples to see how they might manifest.

I wish to find love: you may be asking to find a soul mate or lover, but love comes in many forms. You may get a pet, find a new friend, or have friends who appear in your life and help you through a crisis. Someone may gift you with pink crystals, or you may receive love from guides or angels. In this instance, you need to state that your intention is to find a romantic life partner or to find self-love.

Sometimes you might be presented with the very issue that is holding you back from finding love, and this usually stems from your self-esteem. If you do not love yourself, do you think your vibrational match will be someone who also cannot love you for you?

I would like more abundance in my life: again, abundance can come in many forms. You may receive an abundance of friends, presents, money or love. If you are currently not receiving abundance in your life, ask yourself if you are open to receive. Do you knock back help when it is offered? How do you accept compliments? Are you sceptical of anything? These are all signs you are not open to receiving, so before starting with an abundance grid you might want to create a grid with helping you to open up to receiving. This will bring to light all the areas in your life you want to change to allow for the universe to provide you with abundance. Doing this first could naturally open you up to abundance.

Keeping a gratitude diary is another awesome tool when working with abundance. The more you recognise what you are grateful for the more things will come into your life you can be grateful for. What you put out you receive back. If you are grateful, you are sitting in a higher vibration than that of feeling 'poor me'.

I would like success in my business: the universe provides to those people who know what they want. If you don't know what success for your business looks like you need to work that out first, or you might just go round in circles and never get anywhere.

There is, however, something wrong with all of the issues I have listed above that you might want to manifest. Here's the secret. What is the biggest reason your manifestations don't work? Write this down somewhere to help you to remember, because this is the missing key:

You attract what you are.

Let that really sink in: you attract what you *are*. Think about the days when you are all loved up and everything just unfolds in the most amazing way all day, then think about the days where you woke up feeling less than average due to a bad night's sleep and the day progresses from bad to worse until you go to sleep and start the next day afresh. It all comes down to the energy or vibe you are putting out. I know when I have low health days it's best to stay away from the outside world and tell myself it will pass, because even though I can't help the energy I am putting out I know that it will attract a difficult day.

You are probably thinking it's hard to feel abundant when you are drowning in debt, living from pay cheque to pay cheque and only just getting by. I totally understand this and, yes, it can be extremely difficult, but test the waters and see how changing your inner dialogue and energy manifests big changes in your life.

Remember the saying: 'As above, so below; as within, so without.' This means that your internal environment is a reflection of your external environment and vice versa. What you create on the inside will become your outside. I find that when things are chaotic in my life and I crave peace and want to escape, I need to remember that if I create peace within myself then everything else tends to calm down around me – just like my peace crystal grid card.

Scolecite is a beautiful crystal to find your peace. Notice how the scolecite is in the centre of the grid: it represents you and the centre of your world. It is surrounded by a circle of tree agate, which represents finding peace within and calling on the protection of the tree spirits. I love working with tree energy, and bring these energies to my grids when I require strength and stability. If you are seeking more information on working with trees, look into the Celtic tree calendar and tree Ogham; this is a great place to start.

If you remember that you attract what you are, it's then important to create your intention statements in the present tense as though it has already happened. This is especially important when you start creating your grid and

INTENTION (FUTURE TENSE)	REPLACE WITH (PRESENT TENSE)
I wish to find love.	I am loved.
I would like to find an answer to ...	My questions are answered.
I want to bring a more harmonious flow into my life.	My life is harmonious.
I feel I need protection from negative influences.	I am protected.
I would like more abundance in my life.	I am abundant.
I need help with finding the right career.	I love my career.
I need the courage to leave my current situation.	I am courageous.
I would like to get my creativity flowing.	My creativity flows with ease.
I would like to work on increasing my spirituality.	I am a spiritual being.
I would like healing for a specific health issue.	I am healthy and feel amazing.
I would like success in my business.	My business is a success; I love my successful business.

meditating on your intention. I will take you through this meditation shortly and believe me, it is a powerful practice.

Let's take a look at how you can rephrase your intentions:

You can feel the difference when you read out the present-tense statements. Notice the present statements are about 'I am', meaning you *are*. When you get to the meditation and ritual part you will understand the reason behind this even more, because it is a very powerful tool and is essential for your manifestation to work.

THE LAW OF ATTRACTION

Most people have heard of and understand the law of attraction, which governs *everything*. Every single thing you do in life, every person you meet, every circumstance in every situation comes about because of the law of attraction. Even the reason you are alive and how your physical body has manifested has to do with this law. Karma is also the law of attraction.

Think of it as a pendulum swinging back and forth. Your thoughts and feelings are what make it swing out, and because of this initial energy push it then swings back to you so you can receive. If you fully understand this you can then learn to use it as your guide to creating your reality, which is why you need to put so much thought into your grid. I want you to see how every single thing you do has an effect, and the more thought you put into choosing the right crystals, colours and even your wording the more potent will be the energy you draw to the grid and send out to the universe. Can you imagine just grabbing a few items, placing them randomly somewhere and then expecting them to bring you what you want? No. It may bring you something small, but it will never have the effect of putting all your thought and work into something. This is why ritual work can be so powerful.

You don't really need any tools at all to manifest, as you are the creator of your own reality. Manifestation with crystal grids is a fun way for your mind to understand, and it helps you to focus on the present. The act of any ritual increases your ability to manifest, because it raises a lot of energy to send your intention on its way and it talks directly with your subconscious. It also allows you to connect with your guides, elementals, deities and whoever else you call upon. This is all a part of connecting and learning that there is no separation. The more you connect and respect all the other energies around you the more you will ultimately connect within yourself. Where our attention goes energy flows. The more attention you give something the more energy you are sending it; the more energy you send it the more energy you will receive back. The law of attraction!

INTENTION SETTING

You will now understand why it is vitally important to be clear with your intention for your grid. Intention setting or success planning is how you define exactly what you want in your life.

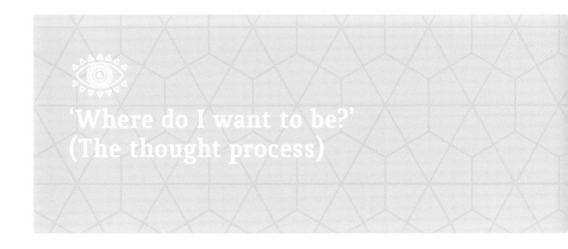

'Where do I want to be?'
(The thought process)

Intention setting is essential in any work you do. I regularly use this to define my business, what I want to achieve, who I want to help and where I want to be. You can apply this to literally anything in your life, and it's good to revisit it each year. I usually start on it before the end of the year so I can start the new year with a strong focus on what are the most important things to work on for the year ahead.

This is why I find journalling so important. You need to ask yourself questions and answer them honestly. When I am stuck, I write out a whole lot questions and then sit down and answer them without thinking too hard. Write the first thing that comes out. Below are examples of what I use for business planning and how to get clear on what it is I need to be doing:

◊   What am I passionate about?
◊   Why do I do what I do?
◊   What do I fear about doing this?
◊   If money weren't an issue, what would I want to be doing?
◊   Who do I admire?
◊   What is it about them that I admire and why? (This will help you determine what you would like others to see in you. Sometimes, it's not what you do but why you do it that people are drawn to.)
◊   Why would people like what I do?
◊   What do I want to be known for?
◊   Does what I do help others in any way?

This should bring to the foreground whether or not your heart is in your work. Are you doing something for the money or because you enjoy it; is there something that has come up you love doing that you should be focusing on? Are you in it for the social stature, or are you in it because you want to make a difference and care about others? When you write down honest answers you will get a feeling from them. If you write what you are passionate about and aren't aligning what you do to that, are you following your purpose? If you do something for the money only, will you be able to keep up the motivation to do it if your heart isn't in it? Look at the reasons why you admire certain people: is it for their talents or their fame or how they make you feel?

Look at how these qualities are reflected in yourself, and see how you can bring these qualities to your work. Ask yourself what you want to leave this world when you are gone or if you are happy to just enjoy a beautiful life. Most important when working in business is asking yourself how what you're doing helps your customers. If you don't know how your business or product can help your customers you could brainstorm what kind of customer you want to attract and what kind of issues you see them facing that your product could help with.

The big question around 'What do I fear about doing this?' can give you some extremely helpful advice, whether you ask this around your business, health or love. This is usually the road block to what is holding you back from achieving your goal. Your fear might be a fear of success, of failure, of it not being sustainable; people might not like what you have to offer or think you are weird. Your fears will sometimes hold you back from perceived ideas of what can happen, so they are a great place to start with manifesting or giving you an indication of what you need to work on. They are the key to getting what you really want.

It's important to ask yourself the bigger picture questions as well: what does success look like for me in five years' time? This is a vitally important step. Placing the timeline five years into the future takes off the limitations you might immediately think of as being unachievable in such a short amount of time. Placing things five years into the future allows you to really visualise what you would love your life to look like. Start with your perfect day, which might go something like this:

> I wake up each morning of my own accord, kiss my partner good morning and we both get up. I eat breakfast outside overlooking my beautiful property while my partner heads off to work. I get started with what I have to do for the day, working in my home office at the computer writing books and creating artwork. I feel happy and content and enjoy a variety of tasks in a peaceful and calm manner. I love that I am able to enjoy working from home and get to make a difference in people's lives. I am so grateful for the life I live and the abundance it creates. I have the money I need to create what is needed, and live comfortably and holiday somewhere new every year. My partner comes home after work and we have a beautiful dinner outside with a glass of wine. We head to bed, ready to start another day feeling happy and grateful.

I have not specified exactly what I do or how much money I earn. I have created a vision with *feeling* and *emotion*. I am 'happy' and 'content' and my environment is 'peaceful and calm'. I am 'grateful'. This makes for an extremely powerful intent when you get to your meditation because you attract what you *are*. It's about defining your goal in the present tense, and you can see that by writing out this statement you essentially create a paragraph of intention in the present tense.

Let's take a look at manifesting love using the same technique:

> I love waking up each morning next to my loving, caring, gorgeous partner. I feel so in love and so content. I love how connected we are; I love how in love we are. I have such a sense of peace within me now knowing that I am with who I am meant to be with. Being together makes me so happy, and every moment we spend together I cherish. I am so grateful for this gift.

OR

I love how content and happy I am. I love that I love myself and who I have become. I am grateful for the love I feel for myself and the peace it brings. I feel relaxed and in the flow of love. The more I love myself, the more love flows to me.

OR

I love the feeling of love that surrounds me. I love walking into my home and feeling loved. It feels peaceful, relaxing and happy. I feel content and grateful for this loving home I have created.

When it comes to health, I tend not to use the words 'cured of illness', as sometimes illnesses or conditions are incurable. I do believe in miracles and the incurable being cured if you have the mindset and determination to manifest this, but keep in mind that some people are not at that level yet and your thoughts and beliefs must align in order to achieve it. If you firmly believe you can be cured of your illness then by all means manifest away! If you have the fear or the belief that you can't, please start off with something that feels right for you. It may be easier to learn to live with an illness and understand it to learn your limitations from it.

There are people who have learned to live with their condition and do what others have told them they would never do; they are an inspiration to others. Sometimes it's about learning how to adapt to and excel at what you have been dealt. There is always a reason why an illness is acquired, so it may be better to ask to learn the lesson of why you have it or learn to live in peace with it. Here is a health manifestation:

I wake up each morning feeling peaceful and calm. I listen to what my body needs for the day and give it what it needs. I feel healthy and well and at complete peace. I feel grateful for all the lessons my body teaches me and am at peace with where I am in my life.

OR

I am in awe at the lessons I learn and the people I meet on my journey with my body. I love my body and who I am. The more I listen the more I learn.

You may feel that you don't have time to take it easy because you have so many things to do and it just isn't possible. This is another road block. The power of these statements is to leave all the reasons *why* you can't do something behind. It's about putting yourself into your future body of where you want to be, not about where you are now and why you can't do what you want to do. That's why I have set the limit at five years: you'll be amazed at what is achievable in that time, and these exercises are about manifesting what you want. The manifestation part and the spiritual work that helps you to achieve your goal is usually way beyond your comprehension, and you need to leave yourself open to any possibilities you currently aren't aware of.

Make sure you set your intention for positive, not negative: you need to be aware of what you are asking for. It is very important to get your terminology correct. If there is something you don't want, *don't* write 'I don't want' in your intention statement. For example, if you say 'I don't want any more negativity', you are putting the word 'negativity' out to the universe and a strong emotion of not wanting something behind it. The law of attraction will attract to you what you are putting out, so you need to put out something such as: 'I am positive and I am protected by love', at the same time feeling you are surrounded by positivity and protected by love.

Don't say 'I don't want to forget'; say 'I need to remember.' You always want to send out positive actions, so no matter how it comes back to you it will always be positive.

One thing you must **never** do is try to manipulate anyone. If you are in love with someone and want them to love you, you cannot try to manifest this. The universe always knows what is best for you, and if that person is not in love with you there is a reason for it even though it may not feel like it at the time. You need to manifest the person best suited to you, which will allow for all the possibilities you have not thought of or do not know are coming to appear in your life.

EXERCISE

Look at one key area in your life you wish to manifest. If you are not quite clear on what this is, write in your journal some questions to answer.

See if you can work out what chakra your issue may relate to. Go back to Chapter 4 or take a look at what colours you wrote down that you love or dislike; this may give you a clue!

Write out a paragraph of your perfect day in five years with regard to what you want to manifest and set your grid up to do. You will be using this in Chapter 8.

MOOD BOARDS

Mood boards: yes! You've probably heard about these before, and until I actually used one with my keys to manifestation they had never worked. This is really an optional step, but I was amazed that each of my images on my mood board actually came to be. Once I had ticked off everything on it I started on my next one. It did take about three years for everything to manifest, but I had some pretty big goals: love, a home, my oracle cards to be printed, to become an author, to travel, and I snuck a picture of talking at the mind/body/spirit festival on there, which I thought was a little out there but achievable and it came true.

Once you have done your success planning and intention setting, you have created an alignment with your beliefs and your intentions. Next you do the meditation, which pulls everything together. Your mood board serves as a visual reminder to keep your intentions going, then after they are all manifested it serves as a tool to confirm what you are capable of achieving.

If you are not familiar with mood boards, I say it is a good thing to prepare once you have some intentions and five-year plans. I do mine on the computer and drag images from the internet into an A4 document and print it out. You might grab some magazines or even draw what you want on yours. It doesn't have to be a masterpiece; just make it yours, and try to put as much feeling into it as possible. If you want to manifest a home, put in an image that looks like the kind of place you would want to live. If you are trying to attract love, put in an image of a couple together that is a silhouette instead of actual faces. Put words on there as well. I placed on mine: love, author, workshops and mind/body/spirit festival. Be creative and have fun doing it! It shouldn't be a chore if you are putting the right energy into it.

HOMEWORK

Try being aware of your thoughts and speech throughout the week and see how many negative words or thoughts you put out compared to the positive thoughts. Take notice of how others speak, and see if you can understand how they are drawing to them what they are putting out. There's no need to bring it up with anyone you observe, as some people can take offence about matters such as this. Just use it for your own learning.

Try to come up with a manifestation statement; it can be as long or as short as you like. Make sure it is to the point of what you want, and that it reflects positivity and can harm no one.

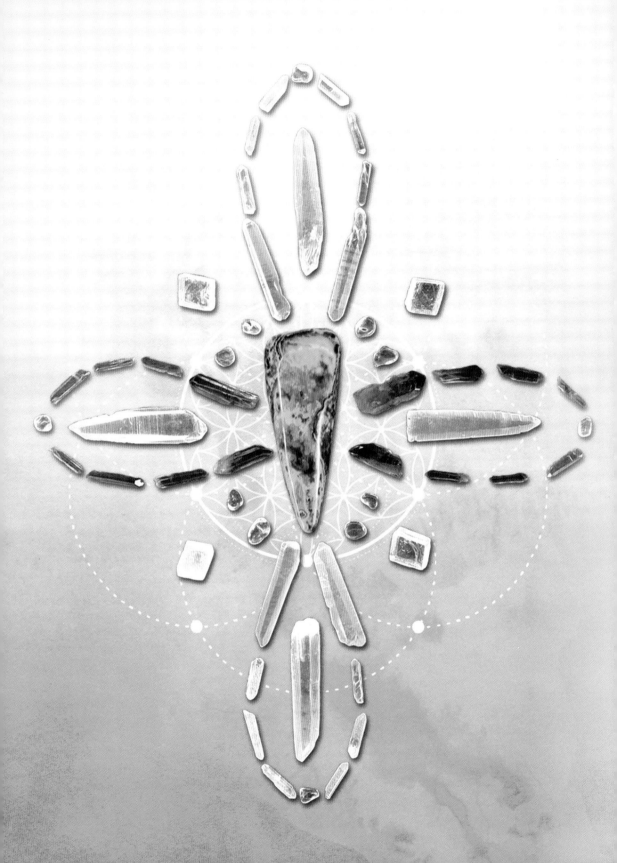

CHAPTER 8

CREATING YOUR CRYSTAL GRID

Here is a checklist for creating your grid:

◊   What do I want to manifest?
◊   Which chakra colour does it relates to?
◊   What stones could I use or what colours do I need?
◊   What kind of grid will I use or will I create it intuitively?
◊   My five-year intention is . . .
◊   Are there any other nature elements I would like to add to my grid?

I have a little process I have discovered with activating grids that I use my pendulum for, so I want you to obtain a pendulum if you can. Don't worry about getting anything extravagant; I use a single terminated quartz crystal necklace on a chain. If you can get a quartz one that's great, but if not be guided by intuition and see what you can manage. See what jewellery you have that might work, or see if there is anything you can make yourself.

Got everything? Great! Let's get started on making a potent grid and get your intention out into the world.

PLACEMENT OF YOUR GRID

The placement of your grid is dependent on a few things.

Where do I have space for a grid that won't be disrupted by children or pets? It is important to have an area that will not be affected by eager toddlers or pets. In saying that, pets are sometimes drawn to grids because they sense the energy from them. They may lie next to them, which is totally fine, but they may also knock stones out of place. Don't be too concerned about this; just put everything back in place and, if you feel you need to, activate it again. (We will be going into how to activate your grid soon.)

Keep in mind it is sometimes good to put your grid where your attention is drawn to it. Where attention goes, energy flows. If you have to walk past it every time you go to the kitchen, for example, you will be giving it more attention and keeping it active. If you put it in a place that is so out of the way even you forget it's there, the energy of the grid may wind down a lot quicker.

If you have an altar, this may be the only place you are able to put your grid. This is totally fine, because you will already have a lot of energy centred around your altar to help activate your grid further.

The best thing to do when trying to work out where your grid should go is to go by feel or intuition. You may get a feel for where it is to go or picture it in a specific spot. Be guided by this insight. You may feel after a few days that it needs to be in a different spot. This may mean that it has done its job where it was and now it needs to be somewhere else.

I find my coffee table works well to create an atmosphere, but I also use a little table next to my bed as an altar where I put my special things. I create grids there that I know won't be disturbed and use them to meditate with. Sometimes I create grids to sit in when I am home alone to do my journeying or meditating in. I have made grids outside, which feels very energising and grounding, but I am a very private person so find this a little difficult to do in case someone is watching me. Sometimes I put up a grid for just a short time only. It isn't necessary for it to be up for any length of time, because once you activate it and send your intention into the universe the intent is out there. Take a photo of it or create a gem elixir from it if you can only have it up for a short amount of time.

What type of grid am I creating? If you want to protect your house you will create a large grid around your property, which may be just the act of placing a crystal at each corner. When gridding your property, it is best to use larger stones than you would for a grid inside the house.

If you want to create a specific atmosphere for a room, place the grid in the centre on a coffee table if that works for your space, or perhaps on a corner cabinet facing into the room.

PREPARING A SPACE FOR YOUR GRID

Now you know where your grid is going it's time to prepare the area. What do I mean by prepare? It's always good to cleanse the energy of an area first. By cleansing a space you are clearing away energy and making room for new energy, also called 'making space'.

If you're doing a full room grid, open up all your windows and doors and light some incense or use a smudge stick to clear the air. Let the breeze come through the windows and wash away any residual energy that no longer needs to be there. A thorough vacuum or mop of the floors is good to do as well.

If you are using a table or certain area for your grid, remove all clutter and wipe down all surfaces. If you're gridding your bedroom, remove anything from under your bed. This is also good feng shui, as it allows an unobstructed flow of energy under your bed.

Once you have cleaned and decluttered the area it becomes a great place to cleanse, charge and program your crystals before you use them for your grid.

CLEANSING, CHARGING AND PROGRAMMING YOUR CRYSTALS

Cleansing. You need to cleanse your crystals before you use them, as they pick up energy everywhere they go and you want to ensure that it doesn't obstruct the positive intention you are about to put forth. They also become sort of dormant, so cleansing them will wake them up or bring their awareness to this time and space.

There are many methods you can use for cleansing crystals; choose whatever suits you, your space and your crystals:

◊ *Sunlight or moonlight:* leave your crystals in sunlight or moonlight to charge or cleanse them.

◊ *Burying them in the earth or laying them on the earth:* remember where they are if you bury them! You can also put them in pot plants if they are regularly cared for – the plants will also benefit.

◊ *Cleansing in sea water, running water or salt water:* some crystals such as quartz can be soaked overnight in water or just held in a running stream of water to flush away the unwanted energy. Selenite and some other crystals should not be put in water as they can dissolve. Always do a little research first.

◊ *Sound:* using Tibetan bells or bowls, tuning forks, mantras and so on. You can put crystals in your Tibetan bowl when you use it or run a bowl, bells or fork over the crystals. I prefer this method, as it is much easier to do many crystals at once. I find when I do healings that sound helps to let Spirit know I need their attention.

◊ *Breath:* blowing a breath over your crystal as though blowing away the energy is great to use when you have nothing available to you or you want to keep it simple. Intent is key here. Picture and feel the energy blowing away from the crystal.

◊ *Smudging:* gently blow smoke using a smudge fan or feather over the crystals. Smudging is an important tool used in many cultures around the world. I urge you to find what is native to your area that is suitable to use as a smudge stick. It is so important with your spiritual practice to consider the environmental impact of everything you do. White sage and palo santo have been over-harvested due to the increase in demand for them. Many other plants and herbs that you can even grow yourself are suitable to create your own smudge, and just think of the energy it will hold for you if you grow it, learn to attune yourself to it and respect the plant and ask if you may use it for your rituals. Start with growing lavender or sage. Mugwort, rosemary and peppermint are also good. It is up to everyone to do their part, and working with herbs is rewarding.

◊ *Salt:* salt is cleansing because it is highly absorbent. Again, like water, some crystals can be damaged by placing them directly in salt, so I find it best to put your crystal on a small dish and place that in the salt.

◊ *Fire:* placing your crystal in the centre of a circle of candles or next to a candle can also benefit your crystals. I find that fire can cleanse and charge at the same time, because it both creates and destroys.

I find that using Tibetan bells is the best for me, because I can do all of my crystals in my house without having to move them but also won't damage any of them. When I am doing a ritual, I use my smudge stick.

Charging. Charging your crystals gives them a good energy boost so they are at their best vibration to work with – just like it is always best to use fully charged batteries in appliances. Again, there are many methods you can use:

◊ *Sunlight or moonlight:* just as the sun and moon cleanses your crystals, so do they charge them. Edmund Harold says that quartz is not charged by sunlight, only moonlight; I'll leave that one up to you to decide.

◊ *Clusters:* placing crystals on top of clusters is a good way to charge them.

◊ *Crystal circle:* place your crystals in the middle of a circle of cleansed and charged quartz points all facing them.

◊ *Elements:* you might want to place your crystals in the centre of a circle that you create with the four elements, like a medicine wheel grid in itself. At each of the four points of the circle place something that represents each element, such as a candle to represent fire, a bowl of water or a shell to represent water, a feather to represent air and a stone or soil to represent earth. Call on each element to help charge your crystals.

◊ *Love:* I believe another way of charging a crystal is to send it love. Who doesn't feel charged after receiving love? This is especially so when working with quartz, because it amplifies what you send it. Send it love and it will amplify this energy.

◊ *Intent:* I cannot emphasise this one enough. When I charge my crystals I talk to them. I call on them to please be present and let them know my intent is to charge them with as much energy as needed for my purpose.

Programming. Programming your crystals is another important part of your crystal grid if you want it to pack a punch, as it gives all the crystals a unified purpose. There is no one way to do this, so go with what feels right for you. If you feel silly programming your crystals it won't be effective.

You can program all of your crystals at once; there is no need to do each one individually, which would be quite a timely exercise. However, if you want each crystal to have a different purpose then you will have to program each one individually.

Again (and always), intent is the key here. You may have your own way of programming your crystals, but here is what works for me:

◊   You can project an image or feeling of what you want to achieve at the crystal from your third eye.

◊   Verbally state your intent. You can specifically ask the crystal spirits to help you with your intention.

◊   Think of your intent and blow this onto and into your crystal.

◊   I like to connect to the crystal through my heart; I ask for it to please help me and state my intention.

◊   Meditate with your crystal and go into it and state your intention.

◊   Send your intent through your giving hand (usually the one you write with).

◊   You may also like to dedicate your crystal to helping with your higher purpose and to working with love and light.

A heart connection is vitally important for connecting with any being, whether it be human, animal, crystal, plant or guides. It is called the universal language of love because all beings respond to love. It is your heart centre that communicates with the world. Love is the guiding force in the universe, and is how you find your connection back to Source. When you live in a world of love you feel connected to everything; it is magical and inspiring and will make you happy.

EXERCISE

Take 15 minutes out of your day to try this quick exercise. Cleanse a crystal you feel drawn to, then calm and centre yourself and project love to your crystal. You may picture a beam of pink or green energy coming from your heart to the crystal, or just try and project love from your heart to the crystal by admiring it and letting it know you love it. Keep projecting love for as long as you can, five minutes minimum.

The aim is to allow the crystal to magnify your love and send it back to you. You may get any number of sensations, and the experience may even make you teary as you experience the beauty of the sensation. Record your experience in your journal. What kind of emotions did you feel? Could you feel any form of energy exchange? Could you sense the crystal energy wanting to connect with you? Did you see any images or colours? Really be honest. Did you not experience anything? Did you feel as though you were trying too hard to make something happen? Did you feel silly doing it?

It doesn't matter what you felt, saw or didn't feel. This exercise is about helping you understand and getting you into the practice. Try it with other crystals or even try looking at yourself in the mirror and giving yourself love. Sometimes when you don't feel anything, it can mean you are not receiving, or you might be avoiding feeling. You might be too in your head. It doesn't mean you can't feel; you just have to keep trying and working on it.

THE CRYSTAL GRID RITUAL

Get out your checklist and make sure you have everything. There's nothing worse than getting half way through and going: 'Oh, I forgot something!', then running away and coming back to it, which can get you out of the zone you were in. There is a homework task at the end of the chapter you might want to record in advance.

Make sure you have at least 30 minutes for your crystal grid ritual. You don't want to be rushed, and you want to be able to stay in the zone for the whole time. Set your phone to silent so you won't be disturbed. If you need to cleanse your area again, do so. Some people like to have a bath or shower first and have a particular outfit they like to wear. Bare feet or having no shoes is also good for connecting and grounding to the earth.

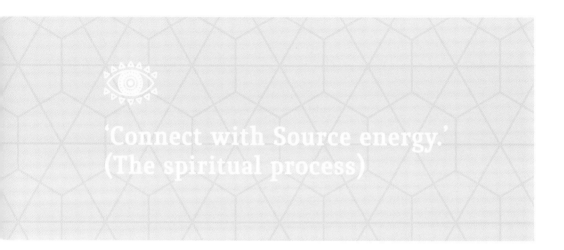

'Connect with Source energy.' (The spiritual process)

Ritual is merely a practice that helps you bring your attention into the present moment and focus on your intent. There is no wrong or right way; it's what you make it. It can be as simple or as elaborate as you like. Don't be limited by what you think everyone else does. Ritual needs to be something you feel comfortable doing, and if you feel silly it won't be as effective as doing something your whole heart and soul is in. *Intent is the key here.*

If you are into spellcasting, you may want to cast your circle and work within it. When I am about to do any form of spiritual ritual or journeying I put on my special pieces of jewellery and my medicine bag with crystals and herbs in it. I might also put a feather in my hair and I have all my crystals ready. I keep my notebook next to me so I can write my experience down straight away once I have finished. No matter what religion you belong to or ritual you draw from, make it yours. Even if you have nothing to do your ritual with, it is your intent and your personal power that make it powerful.

Here's my order of doing things:

◊ *The tree of life:* as previously mentioned, it is always best to start with the tree of life exercise to ensure you are grounded before you begin.

◊ *Smudging:* I smudge myself and my space. Smudge under the soles of your feet. Behind your back is a little tricky, but do what you can. Focus the intent on cleansing any unwanted energy from your body and space.

◊ *Calling in Spirit:* it is important to make your energy known to the space and any other beings that may be working with you or decide to work with you for this intention. You may want to call in specific deities, the elements or just your guides to work with you. I call in the elements at each direction of the medicine wheel: fire, water, earth and air. I then call on the great spirit and then Mother Earth, which is the above and below. You might do this part with your smudge still lit in each direction. I call on my guides, my animal spirits and nature spirits to aid me in my ritual. I ask them to be with me, to help me, to guide me, to teach me.

◊ *Drumming:* I sit and do some drumming, but you could sing or dance. Drumming is known to help drop your brain waves into an altered state that is conducive to meditating and doing ritual work. Singing and dancing can help build energies within your circle. If you don't have a drum you could download a drumming app or listen to some form of relaxing music. The aim here is to immerse yourself into the ritual.

Now you are ready to make your grid.

Step 1. Place your grid template on whichever surface you have chosen, if you have decided to use a template.

Step 2. Place your main crystal in the middle of the grid. You always want to have your biggest stone in the middle and the smaller ones on the outside to start with. You'll end up getting a feel for what works the more you make grids. You can also write your intention on a piece of paper and place it under your main crystal if you want to.

Step 3. Place all of the smaller stones radiating out from the centre stone. You need to consider a few things:

◊   Do you want the energy to radiate out into the room, or do you want the energy to be focused on the main crystal?

◊   Remember the way in which energy travels through a quartz point? That is the direction of energy in your grid.

◊   Pointing crystals towards the centre crystal will amplify the centre crystal's energy. If you choose to grid your bedroom and have a big chunk of black moonstone as the centre stone, you might want to point all your crystals towards it to increase the energy of this stone. Alternatively, if you have the crystals radiating out from the centre stone towards the corners, you might like to have some black tourmaline in each of the corners to increase the energy.

◊   If you have a circle, you might want to point your crystals in the same direction to form the circle so the energy just keeps following the one direction, just like you would in the infinity grid.

◊   If you only have tumble stones and no quartz points, you can place these anywhere.

Step 4. Once all the crystals are in place, it is time to activate your crystal grid.

'A pendulum can show you the
energy direction of the grid and
whether or not it is activated.'

ACTIVATING YOUR GRID

What is activating your grid all about? You might have heard about it or seen some YouTube clips on it and notice that everyone uses a wand to draw an imaginary line between each crystal to link them all up. What I have come to realise is that when we work with crystals we are working with highly intelligent spiritual forms. If you have been following the steps in the book with cleansing, programming and setting everything up and the ritual procedures, you will find that your crystal grid may already be activated. Because you have called in all the helpers you require you have already made your intent clear to the crystals by programming them and, thus, they already know what they need to do.

I have found that a pendulum can show you the energy direction of the grid and whether or not it is activated. It can also activate it, charge it and let you know if there is something that might need moving. I use a pendulum in healings to discover which chakras are out of balance and then allow it to balance each chakra. When you hover the pendulum over a chakra it will swing back and forth in the direction of your head to your toes. If the chakra is not in alignment or needs work, the pendulum will either do nothing (the chakra is deficient), circle around (this can mean excess or can indicate that the pendulum is rebalancing or sending energy to that chakra) or swing in a direction that is not in alignment with your head and toes (a chakra imbalance). Be patient and let the pendulum do the work; let it swing, circle or sit doing nothing if it needs to, until it finally swings in the direction that shows the chakra is once again back in alignment. Here's how I use mine to activate grids:

◊ Hold the pendulum about 10 cm above the main, centre stone.

◊ If the pendulum just hangs and does nothing, keep it there until it moves. This can take some time, so be patient and make sure your arm is comfortable!

◊ After a while it will start to move back and forward along the lines of the energy flow. It might do this for a while then it will move on to the next line, which might be right to left depending on where your stones are. Here's an example:

◊ The pendulum will continue to follow these lines and move on to the next until it has gone around the whole grid.

I have tried this method time and time again and it works every time –
except once. I created a grid and intuitively felt as though something wasn't
quite right. I checked with the pendulum and there were two stones the
pendulum would not flow in the direction of. I changed these crystals to what
I thought felt better and repeated the pendulum exercise, and then it worked.
I find this practice really gives you confirmation of what you are doing and
the help that is coming through for you.

Now that you have activated your grid, it's time to connect to it and send
out your intent.

CONNECTING TO YOUR GRID

When I use any grid that has a particularly large crystal in the middle, I connect
to it by placing my receiving hand on it. This is usually the hand you *don't* write
with. I place my focus on this connection and picture the energy from the crystal
flowing into my palm. I feel the energy travelling up my arm. I feel connected to
it and send it my love, and talk to it in my mind as I would talk to a person. I ask
for it to please help me with my intent and I also perform the last exercise while
still in ritual (record this to play to yourself if you can't remember it all):

*Close your eyes and calm your breathing. Start to connect to your grid by sending
love straight from your heart towards the grid. Picture it as clearly in your mind
as you can. Picture your grid is connected by invisible threads of bright light with
energy flowing through each crystal. See an aura around each crystal radiating out
from them. See these auras all overlapping one another and interacting together.
See that each crystal is connected to the main crystal by also being in its aura. Feel
your own aura expand. Feel your aura and crystal grid aura combine. Feel what it
is like to be a part of your crystal grid, sharing an energy exchange and all working
together in unity. Ask your grid to please help you with your intention. State your*

*intention with confidence, love and joy. Feel yourself suddenly growing older… five years older. Feel your older self in your now body. Fully immerse yourself in your life in five years' time. Look at your surroundings, and take yourself through your perfect day. (You might want to record your five years' time intention paragraph here.) Really **feel** the emotion you will experience once this has come to be. Feel the excitement, the joy, the love and the gratitude. (Keep recording in silence here for a minimum of two minutes so you can visualise this in complete silence.)*

Picture yourself in space looking back at the earth. It has a massive flower of life grid overlaid on it that is glowing just like your grid, but you see it has a round hole in it that your grid will fit into, just like a key. Picture taking your grid and clicking it into place in the earth grid. Once it clicks into place, the entire earth grid glows with incredibly bright white energy and you feel connected to everything. See an amazing aura emanate from the earth and out to space. See it get so big it encompasses you as it expands ever further into the universe. You can see there is a beautiful golden thread from your heart to your grid. Continue to send love to the entire grid, knowing that you are also sending your love to the earth, which is beneficial for all. Feel a sense of gratefulness come over you. Send your feeling of being grateful into the grids. Send a message of thanks to Spirit, the all that is, for helping you with your intention … for always being with you … for giving you life … for giving you all that you need in this life. Feel grateful for all that you have and feel the sense of peace as you know it has come to be.

When you have expressed all that you wish to express, return once again. You feel yourself coming back down to earth … coming back down into your room … into the seat or where you are laying. You feel back in your physical body. Wiggle your toes and fingers and bring your awareness back to where you are. When you are ready, open your eyes.

Thank all the spirit helpers you called in for your ritual and bid them farewell. Close down your circle if you created your ritual in a circle. Make sure you write down your experience, as this can be a great way to understand it better and remember it.

> 'If you don't know what you
> want out of life, the universe
> can't make something
> magically manifest for you.'

Please know you can create your own version of the above meditation. Just ensure you include the five-year intention setting where you sit in the future version of yourself, and feel what it is like to have already achieved your vision. This is the vital part; it is the manifestation secret. Remember: you attract what you *are*. When you envision yourself in your future self as though it has already come to be, you are emanating all the feelings of gratitude, love, happiness and peace in a present tense that allows you to attract exactly that. I cannot emphasise this enough; do not underestimate the power of this process.

Now you are all done! Your intention is set in motion, and the law of attraction will start working its magic. The universe provides for all who know where they are going. When you start fine-tuning your goals and know what you want out of life, your manifesting will be at its best. If you don't know what you want out of life, the universe can't make something magically manifest for you. Over the coming days or weeks there will be things to start looking out for; this is discussed in the next chapter. However, you might have a few other questions in relation to what to do now with your grid.

How long do I leave my grid up for? How long you leave your grid in place is entirely up to you, but is dependent on what you are trying to manifest.

If you want a quick healing or to send some gratitude to someone you may only leave it up for a day. If you are sending someone healing you may want to leave it up for a week. If you want something to grow and manifest on a large scale you might consider leaving it up for as long as possible. I have left grids up for months at a time. The thing to remember is where attention goes, energy flows, so if you decide to leave it up for a long time it is best to keep recharging it every week or so. Being readily visible helps to keep the positive imagery in your mind and consciousness, which means you are also putting out the energy of what you want to attract.

> 'Everything responds in a positive way to love and attention, and if you neglect something it will withdraw.'

How often do I have to recharge my grid? You don't have to keep recharging your grid to ensure it works. Once your grid is complete you have sent out to the universe that which you wish to manifest, and it will continue to manifest for you in some way, shape or form. The point to recharging your grid is to keep it strong with energy. Edmund Harold believed that the crystal will long to become a part of your world as you try and work with it. When you are not working with it it will go within itself again. The more you send it your energy and love the more it will keep its energy up and spreading outwards. Have you ever felt that a crystal or a crystal grid was dull or lacking vitality? Everything responds in a positive way to love and attention, and if you neglect something it will withdraw.

How do I recharge my grid? You can go through the process with the pendulum again if you wish. Alternatively, you can be creative in how you want to recharge our grid. I love to use my Tibetan bells to help clear any energy from the crystals; this does not clear the intent from them, but it does allow me to leave them undisturbed. I also like smudging the grid as well as using it as a form of honouring the crystal and thanking them for helping me. With large grids I place my hand on the point and connect to the crystal and thank it for helping with my intention, and ask for it to continue its work. The more often you communicate with your crystals as though they are a being, the more you will begin to see how everything is connected. Crystals do have a consciousness; just because you may not recognise them as having the same sort of consciousness as yourself doesn't mean you cannot communicate with them.

You might find that over the time you have your grid up you feel other things need to be added. This could be more crystals, jewellery, flowers or shells. I like to sometimes charge the jewellery in my grids, especially my clear quartz necklace in my love grids. You'll feel the love flow from all the stones you have used in the grid that the quartz has absorbed.

If your grid gets accidentally bumped or some of your crystals move out of place, don't worry. Your intention is already out there working its magic. Just replace everything where it should be, then decide whether or not it needs linking up again.

What else can I do with my grid now it is up? A beautiful way to keep the energy of your grid long after you have used it is to create a gem elixir. Place a small container of water within the energy of the grid. Essentially what you create is a homeopathic form of the grid using water, just like a flower essence.

You could create a grid for a person for a distance healing and send them the gem elixir of their grid to take after you have dismantled the grid. You could also send them a picture of the grid you did for them to meditate with as an added extra.

CRYSTAL GRIDS FOR DISTANCE HEALING

Creating grids for distance healing is a simple case of working through what the person you are creating the grid for needs. *Intention is key.* If you don't want to delve into the particulars of what a person needs, you can ask if you can send healing their way or guidance. Create the grid just as you would for yourself. You might want to place a photo of the person who you want the energy to go to within the grid to help with visualising where the energy needs to go, but make sure you have the person's permission to do so. Never direct any energy to someone without their permission, even if you think it is in their best interest.

When you connect to the grid and visualise the intent in the future, hold the image in your head of the person already having received the energy you are sending and them receiving it and being grateful. It is also important to ask Spirit to send the energy the person needs at this time. Try not to think of what they need; trust that Spirit will deliver exactly what is needed.

HOMEWORK

Journal your observations and feelings throughout the week. Take notice of everything, but don't over-analyse it. Just go with the flow.

CHAPTER 9

EXPECTATIONS AND ACTIONS

Your grid is up, so now what? Do you sit back and put your feet up and wait for everything to fall in your lap? It may work like that for some, but generally it's up to you to notice the signs and take action on them.

RECEIVING

Being open to receiving is just as important as setting your intention. If you are not open to receiving even the smallest things in your life you cannot expect the universe to bring you the large things you are hoping for. It does not distinguish between the small or the big things, but senses your resistance. Just as two magnets can attract one another, so too can they repel each other. The more you become open to receiving the more you will receive. Learn to take a compliment, ask for help if someone offers it to you and learn how to open yourself to receiving. When you start to do this, you may also find an equal balance of giving and receiving; it becomes an interchange of energy that comes and goes with a steady flow. This might allow you to feel more connected to the flow, and you will soon begin to see that with every action you take there is an equal action that comes back.

Something I say to myself often is: 'I am open to receive.' I do this when I get acupuncture or a massage, for example. I used to try and stay awake when I got therapy, but came to realise that this resistance to sleeping or relaxing was in some way not allowing me to receive. As soon as I started saying the statement my treatments became so much more effective. It's a simple but powerful statement and is like giving yourself permission to allow something in. You can see how this would work for abundance, love, healing and career.

WHAT TO LOOK FOR AS YOUR GRID STARTS WORKING

You need to be observant, which is where your journal will be valuable. Did you write down all of your observations over the week? You might find things don't make sense straight away. Write them down anyway and come back to them later; they may just give you that a-ha moment! What kinds of things should you look out for?

◊   A-ha moments, for sure; write them down. Sometimes it will come in the form of a realisation, where everything just seems to make sense.

◊   You might get certain images or have certain dreams that really stick. Anything that seems out of the ordinary, that makes you pay more attention than normal, is a good sign.

◊   You might find someone calls you out of the blue about something you need, or you get an offer for something that just comes out of nowhere. These are signs that the universe is drawing the people or situations into your life needed for what you are trying to manifest.

◊   If you have asked for help with healing a certain ailment, you may notice a book that resonates with you or see an ad for a certain practitioner or therapy.

If it is something that keeps sticking in your mind, if you are meant to take note, it will keep showing itself to you. If you decide to ignore the signs you might come to the conclusion that your grid hasn't worked. Your spirit guides will prompt you to take notice of things, be it numbers, number plates, animal signs or feathers that find their way into our path. Your spirit guides may not be placing items in your path just for you but they are trying to make you notice them; they use the items as a way of communicating to you in a language you can understand.

Taking notice of signs is vitally important, not only because you have asked for help or answers through your grid but because it helps you to connect more and more to Spirit. The more you connect and actively make the decision to do this and keep practising it, the stronger your connection will become. In time you will begin, if you haven't already, an open dialogue with your guides and all other beings around you. It will become second nature, as it always should be. This is a natural thing for everyone to be able to do, so don't think it's just for other people. It can be the start of creating a life that feels truly magickal! When you start to see what you can achieve you will realise that you are the creator of your life.

'How do I get there?'
(The physical process)

If you feel you have not received anything, ask Spirit to give you a sign. It's important to ask for help with anything you are stuck on. Spirit is there to help you, and when you call on it it will bring in your higher self, guides and other beings that are willing to help you.

SUCCESS PLANNING

It's time to decipher what you've received and will continue to receive if you leave your grid up. *Action* is the key. You can receive so many signs and messages from the universe after activating your grid, but it will all be worthless unless you acknowledge it and take action on any items that need your attention. You might have a sinking feeling in your stomach with some of the realisations of what you have to do: this is a good thing! It is your guidance showing you what really needs to be done and what is standing in the way of your goal. Trust your gut. You might have received some great inspiration of what you need to do next, so write it down or plan to make it happen. Sometimes it takes great courage and motivation to make things happen.

If any of those a-ha moments have to do with what you need to do next, *do it*! Start whatever you have a pull towards. If it seems impossible or way out of reach, the key to making it happen is simply starting. You'd be amazed at how much ground you can cover when you really want something, and if you truly want something with all of your being nothing will stop you. You are only limited by your own thinking. It is a wonderful thing to know what you want, put it out there and see how it can come to you in the many ways you never could have thought of. Sometimes the road ahead looks overwhelming, but you have to ask yourself these three questions:

◊ *Is the end goal really where I want to be?* If so, then start. If not, it's okay to change your mind. This will help you to really define your goal, so start back at the beginning and get real about what you want.

◊ *How would I feel if I didn't follow this path to achieve my dream?* Take notice of your feelings when you ask yourself this. If it makes you feel deflated, use that as your motivation to get started.

◊ *What are the rewards of following this through?* The feelings you get when thinking of where you could end up should bring a smile to your face. This is your emotional compass telling you that you are going in the right direction. Again, use this as your motivation to get started.

Where do you start? I'm a list writer: I look at my list to see how long everything will take me to do, then I start prioritising what needs to happen first and what can come later. When you start to create a timeline or plan things start to take shape. It shows you the steps to take in what order, and how long everything will take. Make sure to put realistic timeframes on everything or you'll easily become overwhelmed, which is a great way of bringing things to a halt.

It's also important to make the time needed to take the necessary actions. If you've decided to work on your health and have a plan to start meditating for 15 minutes every day, make sure you take the time to do it. You might want to start with doing something every second day so you aren't trying to do too much and end up quitting too early. Take baby steps if you need to. You might have realised you need to cut down on your coffee or sweets intake each day. It might be too much to do it all at once, so make it manageable. Take out one coffee every two days or substitute with a dandelion coffee, so you have an alternative in your routine until your body and mind adjust.

If you are working on business-related issues you might want to draw up a monthly plan and put in some action goals every week that you need to do to move your business forward. You might have decided you need to network, so on your list you could have 30 minutes each week in which you sit down and do some research or planning for it.

> 'If you want to manifest love,
> there are many places to start.'

If you want to manifest love, there are many places to start. You might have come to realise that it starts with you and how you feel about yourself. What can you do to make yourself feel better about you? How can you learn to love yourself, feel better or look better? It could start with what you need to let go of: hurt, rejection, pain, sorrow, loss. It might also be that you need to find a group or activity that will allow you to find someone. Be guided by what feelings you have around finding love and what you may have received after doing your grid ritual.

Be creative and research what other people do if you need to. Look into courses and books on subjects that interest you. Everything is a stepping stone. There are so many resources available with the internet, technology and social media, so use it to your advantage.

Dream interpretation

Did you experience any dreams over the week that you wrote down? Your subconscious communicates to you through symbols and through your dreams. Sometimes your dreams are just about everyday things as your mind catalogues and processes your daily life, but sometimes you will have dreams that really stand out. You can wake up and find the dream is really prominent in your mind and you may even keep thinking about it during the day. These are great indications that something in that dream needs to get through to you. Keep your journal next to your bed and write down your dreams before you get up. You might start to see a pattern emerging from repetitive dreams.

'The dream-time is a place where Spirit can communicate to you and can be incredibly powerful.'

When it comes to interpreting your dreams, I always pay the most attention to what emotions they bring up in me. Many dreams are merely expressions of your emotions. If you have a dream where you are devastated that your partner cheated on you, take notice of how you felt. Did you feel undervalued, not appreciated or not loved, or did you feel that you were ugly or not enough for your partner? Analysing dreams can pinpoint what is really going on within you during your waking life. If your partner is not showing you enough attention you may be feeling unloved or not attractive, therefore you have a dream that they cheat; this is your emotion playing out on the big screen.

Some dreams are very literal and can have deep meaning for you, so pay attention. Some dreams can come as a warning, while others may be where Spirit talks directly to your soul. You might have a dream with crystals, plants or animals that give you messages. These are important to write down and remember. The dream-time is a place where Spirit can communicate to you and can be incredibly powerful.

You may have dreamed about a particular person or being that has given you a gift or said something to you that you need to remember. You will know when these dreams are significant because you will feel them to be real when you are in them. If you can recognise it at the time of dreaming, try to pay good attention to everything and see if you can interact with them. It is possible you are in another realm of being and are interacting with this being. Your dream state allows you to cross safely into other realms. If you choose to believe this, you can work more with it.

Animal messages

Did any particular animals or insects come across your path? Did any of them do anything unusual for you to pay particular attention to them? Did you come across any feathers?

Animals are amazing messengers, and a Spirit can communicate to you through them very clearly. You might have had a bird in your backyard that you haven't seen before, or noticed an animal in your social media feed that stuck out. They will come to you in many different ways. Take notice of their behaviour. Look up what they mean on the internet or in a book. You can also meditate or journey to discover what that particular animal message has for you. This is a great way of finding out its message, especially if you are unsure of what it was. Ask Spirit to help you understand the message it is trying to communicate if you are not sure what it means. Write it down in your journal, as it may become significant further down the track.

Crystals or colours

If you felt a pull to a certain crystal during the week, pick it up and carry it with you or do some meditation or relaxation with it. This may be your guides pointing out to you what you need, or it could be the crystal itself actually singing out to you. Whatever the reason you are drawn to it your body will instinctively know what it needs, so go with those feelings.

To work with the crystal you felt a pull towards:

◊   Ask the crystal: 'What message do you have for me?'
◊   Thank it for its healing and carry it on you.
◊   Hold it while you watch TV or read a book.
◊   Keep it next to your bed to work with you while you sleep.
◊   Make up a gem elixir with it.
◊   You might find it wants to be added to your grid.

There are so many ways to work with crystals, and if you are the kind of person who really doesn't have much time to do anything with them yet, carry it in your pocket or wear it on you somehow. Find ways that work with your schedule. If you don't have the crystal, you could ask for the crystal spirit to please be with you and give you guidance.

If you found yourself being drawn to particular items of clothing or you bought certain coloured items during the week, look up what they might mean with regards to your chakras. What kinds of emotions do these colours bring up for you? Did you have a dislike of any colour? Be sure to look up those as well. Sometimes the colours you dislike indicate an area that needs work that you may be trying to avoid.

Direct information from your guides

Direct information includes things such as full sentences coming into your head from out of nowhere. You know those times when you know it's not really you thinking of something? These times are sometimes termed 'downloads'. There are many ways in which your guides will speak to you, but we are all very different in how we receive our communication. You can receive information through thoughts, words, images, smell and feel. The more you tune in to the subtleness of these communications, the more you will learn to distinguish between what is your own thoughts and what is Spirit. Some people have full open dialogues with their guides; some do not. Some may be doing it without knowing they are. The more you quieten your mind the more you will pick up; meditation will certainly help you achieve this. Try to work with your clair senses as much as possible and write down anything you receive, no matter how insignificant you think it is.

Numbers

Did any numbers keep recurring over the week that you really noticed? Did you look at the time and notice you were always seeing the same time or that you woke up at the same time every morning? Sometimes you will see recurring numbers such as 1:11, 11:11, 222 or 444 and so on. You might have noticed particular number plates or received receipts or invoices with particular numbers on them. Sometimes the triple numbers are perceived as being angel numbers.

Numbers can be the way in which guides or angels get your attention. They direct your attention to numbers that have meaning for you. They can be interpreted in many different ways, so find a resource that resonates with you. Sometimes they can mean something that only you will understand, so if an interpretation doesn't feel right try to discover the meaning for yourself.

Negative events

I know we tend to think that negative experiences suck, but we also know that everything happens for a reason – sometimes we just don't understand it at the time. One thing I like to do when I don't understand why something has happened, no matter how hard it is, is to thank the universe anyway. Why? Because I know that it must have happened for a reason and that reason will be revealed to me in time. I am thanking the universe in advance instead of throwing back negativity to it for something that will ultimately be for my highest good. The more you learn to go with the flow the more you will feel a part of the flow. The more you let control of your life go, the more in control you will become. You begin to see how everything is connected and will no longer feel you are just a victim of circumstance. Trust in the process.

Take a look at the negative situation and see if you can look at it from another perspective. Ask yourself what this lesson is teaching you, what it may be reflecting in you. If it is about a particular person, ask yourself if you hold this quality in some way yourself. There are so many ways you can decide to look at situations. Sometimes it is best to walk away and let the anger go so you can come back and look at it again with a logical view instead of an emotionally fuelled one. Negative events can help you work with your shadow self, the dark parts of your being you don't necessarily like looking at. There can be great healing in these situations.

IF THE THINGS YOU ASKED FOR HAVEN'T MANIFESTED

You are here to learn the lessons of being human to expand your consciousness. If you were perfect and had learned everything there was to know you would not be here. As you manifest you are given clues and ideas you need to act upon; these are stepping stones to the next lesson. You might never be finished learning in each lifetime so don't stress about how long it takes to reach your destination, because when you get there you will find you then extend your journey.

'Keep working at manifesting, and you will notice how your life can transform in a magickal way.'

Each destination leads us to the next, so what you think you need to manifest now may not be exactly what you end up manifesting. It will be what you need at this moment of your journey or may lead you to something better than what you were originally asking for. Be patient and learn to recognise the signs. Keep working at manifesting, and you will notice how your life can transform in a magickal way.

Sometimes there are things in life that are not for your highest good. Sometimes the very thing you think you need is actually the one thing that will stop you from learning a valuable lesson. If you're poor and wanted to manifest a large amount of money, that money might not teach you how to make money for yourself or how to pull yourself out of the money pit. It might not allow you to follow a life path that brings joy. Sometimes the most obvious fix isn't the answer. Don't get me wrong: if I won a million dollars it would make me very happy. The point is, if something doesn't manifest be sure to analyse and reflect back how it might take you off the path you are meant to be on.

EXERCISE

Let's reflect back on what you might have received since creating your grid. Is there something you need more information on that isn't quite clear to you? Have you done a little research but are still unsure of what your message was?

If you have received a message from an animal, plant, flower or shell but are not sure what it is telling you, the following meditation will help you connect to your item. Record the meditation and replace the word 'item' with the item you received.

Perform the tree of life exercise first.

Take the [item] in your hands if you can. Close your eyes and start to calm your breathing. With every breath out, let go of more and more tension from your body. Feel it drain from your face … your head … your neck … your shoulders … your back … your hips … your legs and feet. When you are fully relaxed, take notice of the [item] in your hands. Ask for the spirit of the [item] to be present with you. Picture in your mind's eye what the [item] looks like. Let any images materialise of where it may have come from. Feel, smell or sense if you can what its energy feels like. As you breathe in, picture yourself breathing in the energy of the [item] through your heart chakra centre, and as you exhale breathe your breath back to it.

Connect to the [item] and keep yourself calm and relaxed. Ask its spirit to please give you a sign or understanding of what the message is. Ask it to help you understand how to interpret its message. Ask for its guidance, teaching and healing. In return, give it your thanks and gratitude. (Leave the recording going for two minutes while you sit with the [item] and gain any insight you can.)

When you have received all you can, give your thanks to the spirit you have been working with. Feel yourself coming back into your room, into the seat or where you are lying. Feel you are back in your physical body. Wiggle your toes and fingers and bring your awareness back to where you are. When you are ready, open your eyes.

Write down anything you might have received or experienced in as much detail as you can. Draw what you saw if it helps. Don't worry if you didn't get much from this exercise; with practise, it will get easier.

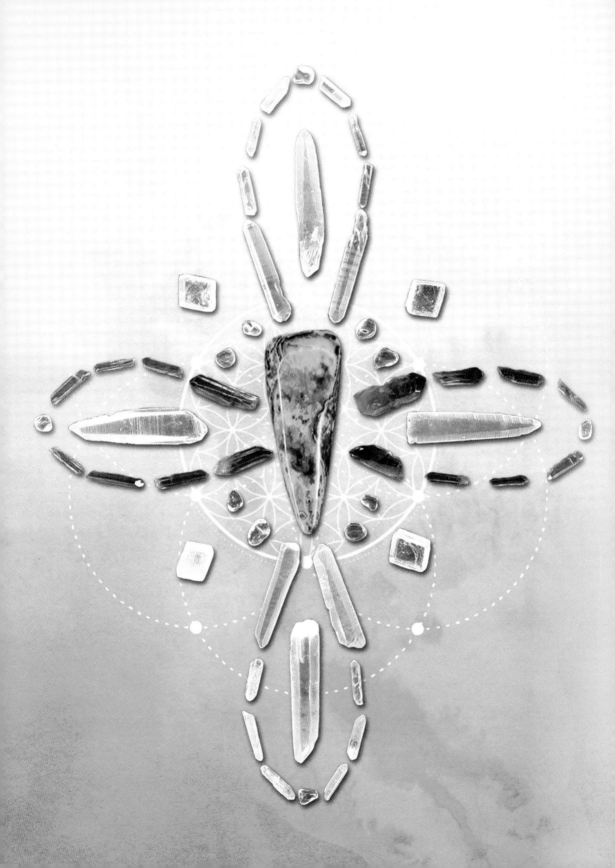

LAST THOUGHTS

Where to from here? Now it's up to you. There is only so far a book can take you, so it's time for you to put it into practice and continue to practise.

Always let intuition guide you. Be as creative as you want to be and inspired by what you have read, and add to what you have learned with your own experiences. Take control and be the creator of your world. Create your own vibrational symphony. When you start to master this form of manifestation you will understand there is no need for any tools at all, for we are all Spirit, we are all from Source.

Crystals and crystal grids serve as a tool to make things easier for you until you have made strong connections or your perception of separation has been shifted. Crystals are amplifiers; they aid your connection to Spirit and are an important tool for your spiritual evolution. You will know when you have reached a certain level of awareness as you will no longer feel the need to obtain more crystals for your collection.

Always respect this connection; you need their help more than they need anything from you. Treat your crystals well, and take heed of the sustainability and ethical sources from where you acquire them. Take only what you need and always lead with an open heart.

I wish you well on your journey, and hope that in some way my words inspire you to chase your dreams.

Nicola x